ENDORSEMENTS FOR DENISE GIBBONS AND 'WOMEN AS LEADERS – THE WORLD NEEDS YOU A PRACTICAL GUIDE'

Denise Gibbons dares to dream: "Imagine a world where everyone is operating from their innate goodness for the betterment of the world and every living being in it, and there are no barriers to participation."

But more than just dreaming, Denise has the experience, intelligence and sensitivity that sets out a pathway through which her dream can be accomplished. In 'Women as Leaders', Denise draws on her own professional career and years of research to explain why the world is in urgent need of more women in leadership roles.

There needs to be a balance. It is a simple fact that women do have a different perspective than men. In leadership, consistency, compassion, empowerment and inclusion often come naturally to women. While often these traits can be stifled in a male-dominated environment, Denise points out how men can be helped to recognise and support development of these qualities in themselves, as well as in their female colleagues.

For women, this book is highly empowering. It celebrates their natural leadership qualities and gives practical advice on how these qualities can be brought to the fore.

I know my own two daughters will benefit from reading this book, as will anyone – male or female – who has an interest in effective leadership.

Dr Ian Gawler OAM
Author of 'Meditation, an In-Depth Guide' and 'The Mind That Changes Everything'

Working with Denise over the past nine years, I have learned a lot about resilience, mindfulness, neuroscience and emotional intelligence. These have been important areas that have facilitated my professional and personal development. Since learning and implementing these tools in my daily life, I feel I am calmer, more confident, and better equipped to understand and work collaboratively with my team and my clients. This book is a wonderful handy guide for all leaders, and contains many of the resources and tools we are successfully using in our business. I have no hesitation in recommending Denise's book as a practical leadership guide.

Samara Badgery
Business Partner, Integrity Wealth

Denise, you truly are an inspirational person, woman and leader in my eyes, and it is evident in the successful business and team environment you've built at Integrity Wealth. But not withstanding that, as a wonderful person juggling many hats in your business and personal life, you've inspired me to want to lead in the same way you have lead me. I found the drive to find out a deeper meaning of how you tick and how this plays and has played a major role in your journey to become a great and inspirational leader, the most compelling. Also, your experiences as a woman in a male-dominated environment and how overcoming these with useful life tools can help young people/women see their full potential and that leadership can be built by them. I wish your ideas on actions to promote women were plastered everywhere for all men and women to see, as I believe like you they need to lead the change in our society. The world needs women! Girl power!

Michelle Christensen
Financial Planner, Integrity Wealth

Denise, my impression of the book is that it reflects how widely you have read and researched, plus how deeply you have reflected upon the issues that you discuss in the book. For me, the most compelling aspects were the parts of the personal journey, which you shared, particularly the challenges that you faced in forging your chosen career. These sections caused me to reflect upon my own attitudes and the path I have followed. To what extent have I been subconsciously biased, particularly towards women in the workplace? Doubtless, getting better outcomes in this area starts with greater awareness and I think your book draws appropriate attention to this. Of course, knowing (only) parts of your story added extra elements of interest for me. It was fascinating to learn other aspects of your journey and to reflect upon the challenges you have faced. With your leadership journey, it's pretty clear that you relished the freedom to lead your way at Integrity. By having your own firm, you were able to create an organisation that reflected a culture, values and attitudes that are integral to your being. Your challenge was to find your path and have the courage to follow that path (without the benefit of a map or a trail blazer to follow). My experience in dealing with you at Integrity has been that you have always led with a quiet dignity and a confidence in going about things your way.

Scott Charlton
Director of Coaching, Slipstream Coaching, and External Chair Board of Directors, Integrity Wealth

I had never thought of myself as a leader in my role as mother until I read Denise's book. It was indeed a gift I wasn't expecting and helped me to recognise different areas of my life where I had been a leader without really noticing that at the time.

Denise is such a warm and caring woman. Her happy outlook on life, as well as her fight for recognition as an equal in the boardroom over the years, is evident as she takes women on a self-discovery journey into the depth of what it means to step through self-doubt and step up to be the leaders they are born to be.

It is indeed a privilege to work with Denise at Transition Planning Australia and I applaud her for the amazing job she has done in setting up and running such a successful business as Integrity Wealth. I am sure that this book will be a valuable source of encouragement for generations of women to come.

Diana McKnoulty
Events and Office Manager, Transition Planning Australia

As people, we are all challenged at times to step up, to speak out, to take the lead.

This usually takes courage, particularly where social customs and culture constrain us. Taking the lead for women has particular challenges and often involves pushing back against societal norms. This book explains the challenges for women in becoming leaders and provides an inspiring, practical guide for women to develop their leadership skills and to achieve their personal goals. This book will help men to "get it"; not just to be aware of leadership challenges for women, but to understand how it is for women who are often placed in these situations.

Neale Condon
Leadership and Management Consultant

Without doubt, I am a better leader for having been in business with and learning from Denise. Through her main leadership traits of Consistency, Compassion, Empowerment and Inclusion, she has taught me what it takes to build and lead a diverse team. Colleagues, team members, clients and the local community are all better off for

Denise's leadership. I hope this book will inspire women to lead and men to encourage them to do so.

Mark Stewart
Business Partner, Integrity Wealth

If you want a lazy read one Sunday afternoon on the couch with a book … Denise's book is probably not for you! If you want a practical and thought-provoking journey on leadership with action, your Sunday afternoon just became more interesting!

Denise takes you on a leadership discovery journey in a very practical way. The book is full of relevant quotes and references that serve to illustrate her points – and infused with examples of Denise's personal journey – both as a woman and leader.

This book is Denise through and through, and reading it is a privilege. I have been part of her journey for five years and can attest to what I have seen and experienced through my relationship with Integrity Wealth. Her willingness to give and share insights into what works and more importantly "how" through her personal experience to inspire others correlates with what I have experienced and read!

James McCowan
Director, Wealth Management Matters

As a mother of two daughters, and an Aunty of three nieces, this is an issue very close to home for me. Having worked as a lawyer for more than 10 years, I have seen the difficulties faced by women on an uneven playing field. Despite rhetoric to the contrary, women remain significantly underrepresented within the upper echelons of "management". There is no "girls club". Giving voice to this issue through your book will hopefully continue the momentum and promote the importance and great contribution that women make in leadership. Asking women to support each other with this challenging journey needs to be emphasised too.

Denise, I haven't worked with you for very long, but I can see that you are amazing at what you do. And you walk the talk. I can always count on you for a kind word of encouragement.

Melinda Shinkel
Administration Assistant, Integrity Wealth

Denise is a true leader and trailblazer and these traits are reflected in her unique book *Women as Leaders – the World Needs You – A Practical Guide*. Denise shares her challenges and lessons learned as a woman in what was then (and is still in many respects?) a man's world, and her book will help to break down the barriers for future women as leaders.

This book is about traditional leadership and much more than that. Women – and men – will benefit from the personal development aspects in the book – knowing yourself, your strengths and what motivates you, and acting accordingly.

In Denise's terms, everyone is a leader – either of a group with a common goal, or of themselves as self-leaders. Self-discovery is therefore important, and we can all learn something from reading this book.

Denise's stated purpose in life is to help make the world fairer, kinder and more joyful. Her approach – to leadership and to life – is very much about helping others and working together for the benefit of our society. This approach is reflected in her book, which is full of practical information and exercises designed to help everyone on their own journey of self-discovery, as part of the process of becoming a better leader – of others and of themselves.

Peter McKnoulty
Consultant, McCullough Robertson Lawyers
Founder, Transition Planning Australia

DENISE GIBBONS

WOMEN AS LEADERS

THE WORLD NEEDS YOU

FOREWORD by DR HELEN SZOKE
Chief Executive – Oxfam Australia

A PRACTICAL GUIDE

First published in 2017 by Denise Gibbons

National Library of Australia Cataloguing-in-Publication entry

Author: Denise Gibbons
Title: Women as Leaders – The World Needs You
ISBN: 9780995446403
Subjects: Leadership in women. Women executives. Women in the professions. Leadership.
This book is catalogued with the National Library of Australia.

Editing, book cover design and formatting services by BevRyanPublishing.com

Disclaimer:
Any information in the book is purely the opinion of the author based on her personal experience and should not be taken as business or legal advice. All material is provided for educational purposes only. We recommend to always seek the advice of a qualified professional before making any decision regarding personal and business needs.

For my beautiful, strong and smart daughter, Evie,
who has enriched my life in so many ways
and helps make my life worthwhile.

CONTENTS

ACKNOWLEDGEMENTS

This book would not be in existence without my book mentor/publisher, Bev Ryan. She has been instrumental in helping me work out my message, my audience and my book structure. She has been my sounding board and my supporter through the writing process. Planning the book launch together was the final catalyst and impetus for me to push through to the end of the writing. Thank you so much, Bev. You are truly a wonderful help. I would recommend you to anyone who wants to write and publish a book.

I would also like to acknowledge my friends and work colleagues who were so excited to complete the questionnaires about leadership at the start of this journey. You gave me a lot of good material for the book.

I would like to acknowledge the people who took the time to be personally interviewed by me. These are Hazel Ruby, Samantha Nyholt, Ranjeet Bassi Cavanagh, Dr Helen Szoke, Jessica Wheelock, Scott Charlton, Mark Stephen and James McCowan.

I would like to make special mention of Hazel Ruby, who

worked with me in the early stages of developing the book. Hazel has written a lovely life story for the book about caring for her father during the final stages of his life. I asked Hazel to tell this story because it highlighted the challenges that women face when they are combining a leadership role and caring for a loved one.

I would like to especially thank Dr Helen Szoke, Chief Executive of Oxfam Australia, who did not hesitate to say yes when I asked her to write the Foreword to my book. I especially appreciate your endorsement of what I hope to achieve with this book.

There have been many people that have been instrumental to my leadership journey. I especially want to thank the team at Integrity Wealth, with special mention to Mark Stewart and Samara Badgery, who have been my business partners through the growth of the business. It is an absolute pleasure to work with all of you. I enjoy our collaborative, fun and inclusive environment. I especially love the dedication, professionalism and care that each of you brings to our clients.

There have been many people who have seen potential in me and encouraged me to continue my career in the financial services industry. I make particular mention to my first business partner, Warwick King, who was a wonderful champion and mentor to me. His encouragement at a pivotal stage of my career ultimately led to the creation of Integrity Wealth. I became a leader through the growth of that business. This showed me the thrill of contribution and the personal satisfaction of achievement through leadership.

I need to acknowledge the support that my former husband,

Orestes (Coco) Gibbons, gave me during our time together. He was always very proud of my career and openly championed me far and wide. This fuelled my confidence to keep going. I would not have been able to build a business and enjoy motherhood without his brave decision to be the stay-at-home carer for our daughter, Evie, at a time when there was a societal stigma on him as well.

There are many friends and colleagues in my volunteering life who have encouraged me to write this book. Thank you for your support and belief in me. I hope you find the book valuable, enriching and practical.

FOREWORD

How many decades have we been talking about equality for women, and how are we actually going? Sure, we have made some inroads into important areas, but this is 2017, and we should have had seismic shifts, not little shuffles.

There is a lot that has been done – legislative changes, policy changes, reporting and recording, setting milestones. We have lots of powerful and famous women who have demonstrated their capacity, and implored us to "lean in" and take the system on. We need all of this.

But this book gives us something more. Denise is one of those women who has challenged the established view, shrugged off attempts to "place" her by virtue of her gender, and has been successful in her own career. And she does what women do best, and what more of us need to be doing – network, connect, assist and support other women in all walks of life. The time is ripe for a practical guide.

In the work that I do for Oxfam, we know across the world that whilst women are often the most vulnerable group in communities, they are also the solutions to the community, family, regional and political challenges that they face. This is also true in our western countries, where we still grapple with providing flexibility in the workplace; creating nourishing and support- ive context for women returning to work from maternity leave; achieving equal pay; and recognising that experience comes in many forms.

I can tell you that this book will be on hand for my own deliberations, for the discussions with my daughters and daughters-in-law, and in the talks I have with many young women who want to know how to progress their work lives. As the title of the book says – the world needs you. We need women to feel confident and empowered. We need women's voices in all walks of life. As the world becomes more volatile and unpredictable, we know that it will be women who make the difference.

Dr Helen Szoke
Chief Executive, Oxfam Australia

INTRODUCTION

He was angry. He was very angry.

His eyes glared at me and his body language stated clearly – "You shouldn't be here". When he spoke to me his words were considered, but his manner made the words shout across to me and clearly indicated that I was not wanted as part of this group.

I was one woman at a table with nine other men. This was the reason for David's agitation. He could not understand why I was there. I guess he had a point, because I was there by default.

It was 1985, and the Institute of Chartered Accountants in Australia (as it was known then) had just introduced a requirement that current members had to achieve 20 hours of structured professional development every year to maintain their membership with them.

A group of smaller firms of accountants had banded together to meet monthly as part of this requirement. The cost of paying for professional development sessions would have been a prohibitive burden for these smaller firms.

I was working on a business contract as an accountant with

a three-partner accounting firm in suburban Brisbane. I mentioned to one of the partners that I needed to ensure I met the professional development requirements too. He advised me that he had been invited to be part of this group but was unable to attend, so he organised for me to take his place.

There were lots of layers to David's resentment that I was seated at that table. I had encountered this type of behaviour many times in my professional career to date.

I was not going to be intimidated by him though because I had every right to be there. In many ways, I was more professionally qualified than many others in the room.

David's attitude predominantly came from the change in dynamic that occurred because I was a woman. He was used to being part of "the boys club", where he could instinctively operate around his known behaviours in that club. A woman at the table meant that he would have to be constantly conscious of what he said and did.

David is an honourable man. However his learning about respect for women and his understanding of where women were expected to be in society, meant that he had difficulty accepting my presence at that table.

At that time, women were still expected to be solely in the private space as homemakers and be a support person to men. Men resided in the public space as businessmen, politicians and leaders in society. There was very little crossover between these spaces at that time.

Of course, I was young and naive and did not fully understand this dynamic. I just believed that I had a right to be at that table and so I was going to be seated and be heard. I was very serious about my career and was prepared to do whatever was required to maintain that career. I was not going to be intimidated by David's behaviour.

I sat at that table with those men for 25 years. When I left the group, I know that every single one of them had enormous respect for me as a professional accountant.

David even acknowledged that I had been beneficial to the group by making them lift their standard of engagement, because I was a woman.

The strange thing is though that I was never fully accepted as a businesswoman. I know that they shared much more between each other than they did with me. I heard them at each meeting discuss how they had interacted with each other by consulting each other on professional issues that arose.

Some of them owned horses together. Some of them referred clients to each other. I was very rarely included in that dynamic and never invited to be part of it either.

They rarely asked my opinion on how to run a business and I was rarely consulted on professional issues regarding clients.

In fact, when one of the men wanted to lessen his workload by offering work to another, this was never even offered to me but instead went to one of the other young men who had joined the group.

Over the 25 years that I was part of this band of accountants, I built a successful financial services business and they were all aware of this.

However, of course, I had made the classic feminist mistake. I thought that just because I was at the table I would be part of the power dynamic that existed within that group.

It is not that simple. It is complicated, complex and challenging for women who want to be leaders.

In my book, I discuss this dynamic more and hopefully provide some methods to change the discourse and processes. I know in hindsight that it would have been better had I acted differently.

I have written this book as a practical guide for young women about leadership, with the hope that it will provide some tools to crack and even shatter that last glass barrier that exists for women – the barrier that keeps us from being part of the power decisions of the world.

I have written this book with the hope that young women, who are doubting their leadership abilities or cannot see the sense in being leaders when they want to be mothers, will see that being a leader is important for their family and their community as well as themselves.

Leadership does not have to be grandiose. It can be as simple as running the tuckshop at school or a book club or a netball team for your daughter's school. When you have a family, sometimes that might be the only form of leadership you can fit into your life.

The skills you gain from these important family and community roles translate into running bigger projects or aiming for corporate boards or becoming a politician should you choose to take these paths.

Leadership can be learned. In fact, I believe, the world needs more training in this important skill. We often believe that leadership will just develop as part of the process of moving up the ranks in an organisation. This is not the case. Management of people is not the same as leadership of people. I certainly wish I had this book when I was starting out in my career.

There is no doubt that the world has shifted and women have many more opportunities in society. The gender stereotype is slowly being whittled away.

However, it is too slow.

We are half the world's population and the statistics show that we are a long way off reflecting this fact in the power centres of the world. Except for a few countries, women are still not equally represented on boards of businesses or cabinets of governments.

In Australia, women compromise 50.2 per cent of Australia's population. However, according to the Inter-Parliamentary Union as of 2 July 2016, the statistics for Australia's parliament show that women make up 28.7% of the House of Representatives and 36.8% of the Senate. Also, in terms of positions of power, there are five women in cabinet positions in a total cabinet of 21.

The Australian Institute of Company Directors states that at 30 June 2015, the percentage of women on company boards in Australia was 20 per cent.

The world faces many challenges in the 21st century. There are climate change, population pressures, and the rise of terrorism, to name a few.

It is going to take diverse teams in business, government and the community to tackle these challenges. Diversification will be required on every level – not just gender. The leaders of the future will need appropriate skills to bring people together to achieve the goals necessary for a better world.

The style of leadership that I believe will be necessary for our 21st century world will be explored further in Chapter 1, entitled 'What is Leadership and Why Become a Leader?'. As a basis, I have chosen the Toastmasters International definition of leadership, from their High Performance Leadership Development Program[1] entitled 'Service Leadership':

> *Service leadership requires the capacity to lead both with a focus on service to those benefitting from the end result and those who do the work achieving the objective. Service leaders are willing to place empowerment above personal power, contribution above their own ego satisfaction and the needs of the team above their own needs for credit and acclaim.*

The skills that women have through their traditional role as the carers of the family translate well into this arena. Women often need to negotiate different ages, genders, nationalities, and religions to keep families together, as well as ensure the well-being of the individuals in the group.

We just need to be able to translate this into the public space while ensuring our families are nurtured as well. Yes, a tall order I know.

The more the world sees authentic, effective and collaborative women leaders, the more it will be acceptable. Perception is everything.

Imagine a world where everyone is operating from their innate goodness for the betterment of the world and every living being in it, and where there are no barriers to participation.

This is my dream.

I want it to be your dream too. The rewards are enormous and compelling.

From a personal perspective, imagine the satisfaction of being part of that change, as well as ensuring that our daughters, granddaughters, nieces have better choices in their lives.

The result I believe is that we would have a world where peace reigns, where there would be no poverty and no wilful destruction of lives and our planet.

In the words of John Lennon:

"You may say I'm a dreamer
But I'm not the only one
I hope someday you'll join us
And the world will live as one."

Women as leaders – the world needs you!

HOW TO USE THIS BOOK

"Enlightenment is intimacy with all things."
Dogen Zenji

I have written this book as a practical guide. I have touched the surface of many topics, tools and concepts that I consider important to leadership. I have also covered some of the challenges that are specific to being a woman leader.

Because it is a guide, I'm hoping that you will carry it with you on your leadership journey as a reference point so that you can undertake your own research into the areas that resonate with you for your own discovery and improvement.

The book is aspirational. I have included lots of the latest scientific studies on human behaviour because I believe we need to become smarter at interacting with each other. I'm hoping that women leaders will show the way.

Most of the stories in the book are from my own life and leadership journey. I would encourage you to seek out other women and discover their stories too. For example, I would encourage you to read or subscribe to inspirational publications such as the digital magazine *Honestly Woman*[2] (www.honestlywoman.com), which is full of stories about strong women and their life journeys.

Becoming an inspirational leader takes a lifetime, and there is much to learn every day. I have tried to break the learning down into bite-size pieces surrounded by large chunks of meaty substance. Sometimes we don't have the time for large amounts of information, but we do have time for the bite-size pieces. Other times we want to immerse ourselves in the learning and experience the wonderment of discovery. We want to experience that moment when our mind expands into enlightenment.

Each chapter starts with the meaty substance and finishes with the bite-size pieces.

Like most things in life, start where you are. Work out what you already know about leadership and what you want to achieve with your learning from this book. It may be that you want to know how to get started or it may be that you want to enhance your current learning.

There are a couple of chapters that I believe you must read first – 'Know Thyself' and 'Know Your Why'. They are, in my opinion, critical first steps.

They provide the foundational building blocks for self-understanding and self-leadership. It won't matter if you are just starting out or if you are further down the track. These chapters form the basis of ensuring you stay on track with your leadership journey.

Learning happens in increments. You discover a new idea that is wonderful. Until you have introduced it into your life and incorporated it into who you are, it is still only a new great idea.

The Aseo tribe in Papua New Guinea, have a saying – "Knowledge is only rumour until it goes into the bones". So, you need to set up a process to make the new wonderful ideas stick and stay in your life. This can be achieved with deliberate practice, which I discuss in Chapter 7, 'Practice, Practice, Practice'. Once it sticks, it is a learning. This simply explains habituation and how to make the conscious an unconscious part of everyday life.

I have recommended purchasing various online tools to assist with "knowing thyself". It is not a great expense, and hopefully you will see it as a worthwhile investment in your leadership and personal future.

I also hope you will join my online community as it develops, and consider some of my leadership programs.[3] My website is www.denise-gibbons.com.

I have set out here the process I recommend for reading the book. If you are someone who just likes to read a book from start to finish, then do that. You may find that coming back to this how-to-guide is useful for your leadership journey.

Create your personal and leadership foundations

Step 1: Read 'What is Leadership and Why Become a Leader?'

Step 2: Reflect on your experience to date around leadership. Determine what you believe is important as a leader and make a list.

Step 3: Read Chapter 1, 'Know Thyself'

Step 4: Read Chapter 2, 'Know Your Why'

Step 5: Undertake the online tools in Chapter 1 to help you discover your unique characteristics.

Step 6: Do the exercises in Chapter 1 and Chapter 2, including reflecting on your shame triggers.

Step 7: Write your 'Life Sentence – your Personal Value Proposition (PVP).

Step 8: Review your list from Step 2 after completing Step 6. Observe if your list has changed and make notes.

Step 9: Start your process of self-discovery by observing and recording how you carry yourself each day. Look at this around your Life Sentence and what you have learnt about your personal and leadership foundation.

Construct your self-leadership structure

Step 1: Read Chapter 7, 'Practice, Practice, Practice'.

Step 2: Read Chapters 3 and 4, 'Knowing Your Playing Field' and 'Know Your Tipping Point'.

Step 3: Reflect on what barriers you may encounter along your way and look at some processes to counter these barriers. Construct lots of "If … Then …" statements to help you stay on track when the barriers appear.

Step 4: Read Chapter 6, 'Basic Skills Required'.

Step 5: Consider what leadership skills you have and what you still need to learn.

Step 6: Read Chapter 5, 'Basic Steps'.

Step 7: Work out the steps for each project for your leadership journey using this tool and apply it to what you have identified in Step 5.

Step 8:   Work out the deliberate practice steps for each project, and work out how you are going to incorporate this practice into your life.

Step 9:   Read Chapter 8, 'A Call to Action'.

Step 10: Work out actions you can take to promote women's issues.

Step 11: Just do it, and remember to enjoy the daring adventure.

Sustain your leadership journey

Step 1:   Read Chapters 9–11.

Step 2:   Work out what steps you need to take in your life to nourish and replenish you as well as manage 'The Big Squeeze'.

Step 3:   Schedule 'me-time' in your diary based on Step 2, and commit to keeping the appointment with your most important person – you.

Step 4:   Schedule regular time for rest and reflection including holidays.

Step 5:   Regularly review your Life Sentence and your leadership successes. Celebrate your achievements.

WHAT IS LEADERSHIP AND WHY BECOME A LEADER?

What is leadership?

The British Dictionary defines a leader as a person who rules, guides or inspires others.

There is little chance that many of us can rule a state, monarchy or country. I am not saying it cannot happen, and if it is your ambition then certainly go for it. It is certainly an honourable aspiration and should be pursued.

For all of us, however, there is every opportunity to guide and inspire others.

For this book, my definition of a 'leader' is:

Anyone who helps or enables others to reach a common goal or solve a mutual problem and holds themselves accountable for this potential and the outcome.

This can be guiding your child through their school years or running a business or a country. Everyone can be a leader if they want to contribute to a group that is working towards a unified purpose.

The characteristics of this style of leadership are best summarised in the definition of Service Leadership. Toastmasters International, in their High Performance Leadership program, summarises Service Leadership as follows:

> *"Service leadership requires the capacity to lead both with a focus on service to those benefitting from the end result, and to those who do the work in achieving the objectives. Such leadership requires working with a spirit and set of values that emphasise worthwhile contributions. Service leaders see their role as enabling or empowering others to accomplish something worthy.*
>
> *Service leaders are willing to place empowerment above personal power, contribution above their own ego satisfaction, and the needs of the team above their own needs for credit and acclaim."* [4]

This definition of leadership places much emphasis on self and the contribution of self to accomplish something worthy.

Some people believe that leaders are born; however, this is not true. We can all lead if there is something we believe strongly in. Leadership can be learnt just like any other skill.

Just think about the skill that is required to encourage your family to go on a family holiday, or to organise a family gathering for an important milestone.

This is leadership.

Why be a leader?

"You must be the change you wish to see in the world."
Mahatma Ghandi

We all want to be happy and live a good life. We all want to feel that our presence on this earth for the period we are here has meant something. This need for meaning comes with human consciousness.

Leadership development promotes personal growth and personal growth leads to life-long personal satisfaction. Does this sound like a win-win scenario?

It is not about glory because on projects there is very little of that. It is not about recognition because this can be fleeting, random and even negative at times.

There is just the overall satisfaction of contributing and making a difference, however small and humble.

Leadership is an "inside-out" process.

Scientists have shown that helping others results in a more sustainable increase in positive emotions than just having fun. Positive emotions are one of the cornerstones for allowing us to flourish in our lives.

When you are happy, engaged and enjoying life, you are at peace with yourself. This flows out to your family and friends. It permeates the community you live in and ultimately into the world. Being empowered strengthens communities and ultimately improves the quality of life for everyone.

By choosing to be a leader, I view every project that I undertake through the lens of helping others. I seek the potential in others for the project I am undertaking. This creates enjoyment, even if it is unsuccessful or incomplete. There has always been someone that has been touched by the process, which has in turn touched me.

In the words of Ralph Waldo Emerson – "To know that even one life has breathed easier because you have lived, this is to have succeeded."

Not everyone can be the leader – self-leadership

It is true that on most projects there needs to be one person who is the ultimate driver, for example, the Chair of the Board of Directors of a company, the co-ordinator of a project to celebrate an important historic event, the captain of a sporting team.

Unless you work in isolation on a one-person assignment, you are required to be part of a team of people and will be responsible for the completion of part of the process for the overall project plan.

If this is the case, then all the leadership skills discussed in this book are just as important for your role as a self-leader. In fact, the success of any project will critically depend on everyone's self-leadership and their reporting to the ultimate leader.

Given the pace of change in our world now, it is impossible for one person to be across all facets of what is required to run a successful project, business or government.

Teams of committed, dedicated and motivated self-leaders are what the world needs.

What this book aims to achieve around leadership

This book takes you through a process of self-discovery about who you are and what you want your life to be. This gives you your path to follow – your true north. Your life path determines what you will bring into your life.

I'm hoping that once you can see your potential and your unique talents, you will want to step out and be a leader for any project that comes your way. I'm hoping that you will feel empowered to speak up for societal changes that are needed to make it easier for women to be leaders, but most of all, to be accepted as leaders.

I'm hoping that you will feel empowered along your journey to support other women and men to step up and speak out for everyone who needs inclusion in our society.

In this book, I discuss many life and leadership tools for you to use on your journey. These are based on my own discoveries and are presented in relation to our human traits and the current scientific information about their benefits. I'm hoping they are useful, and that you will also look for your own tools, as well as stay informed about continued scientific discoveries that will enhance your way.

Remember you don't have to do it all on your own. Make certain you look for good mentors, champions and venting partners to be your guides and supporters.

The world needs you. Enjoy!

Research process for the book

Before writing this book, I asked men and women to complete a questionnaire around leadership, with specific questions about women as leaders. I surveyed 22 women and 14 men.

Some of the results are as follows:

Women's question: If you are currently enjoying a leadership role or would like to be in a leadership role, why does that appeal to you?

Highest results:

- Wanting to make a difference to your community, world or your cause = 66.67%
- Personal development = 57.14%

Question to both men and women: Do you believe having more women at leadership levels in business, government and the community will make a difference?

Women's results: Yes = 95.24%

Men's results: Yes = 76.92%

Question to both men and women: What do you believe would inspire young women to aim for leadership roles?

Mentoring: Men = 88.24%; Women = 45.45%

Strong women role models: Men = 88.24%; Women = 45.45%

Societal change: Men = 58.82%; Women = 45.45%

There were many comments made in these questionnaires by both men and women about what is needed for change. I believe the results above summarise the most important factors, and in this book I have endeavoured to cover issues raised in the research.

I have also shared below some of the thrills and skills of being an inspirational leader that were told to me during my interviewing for this book.

- *Never ever quitting.*
- *Know who you are.*
- *Loving yourself so you can love others.*
- *Studying other inspirational leaders.*
- *Living an inspirational life, and inspiration to me means to inspire others to live their truth in service for others.*

Ranjeet Bassi Cavanagh

- *Sharing your role, glory and recognition.*
- *Trusting people with what you are handing over to them to do.*
- *Empowering people by encouraging them to run with what you have asked them to do.*

Jessica Wheelock

- *Being part of a positive group means you walk away feeling good.*

Samantha Nyholt

- *You can drive the difference you want.*

Dr Helen Szoke

- *Having people invest in the mission that you have created is really rewarding and encourages me to do more.*

Scott Charlton

- *I like the ability to influence and make a difference. Self-doubt happens for me when I'm not making a difference.*
James McCowan

- *Finding team cohesion.*
- *Active, passionate and respectful communication.*
- *Achieving common purpose.*
- *Achieving goals and objectives leads to self-fulfilment.*
Mark Stephen

I hope you find these inspirational in your own leadership journey.

WOMEN AS LEADERS – THE WORLD NEEDS YOU!

STEPS TO GET FROM A STAGE OF DOUBT TO A STAGE OF KNOWING

CHAPTER ONE

KNOW THYSELF

"This above all: to thine own self be true,
And it must follow, as the night the day,
Thou canst not then be false to any man."
Shakespeare – Hamlet Act 1, scene 3

My daughter and I are like chalk and cheese. I am introverted and she is extroverted. I am an academic and she is an athlete. I love being in the mind and my daughter loves a physical challenge.

I'm sure you can appreciate that this is a very simplistic analysis of who we are. My daughter does love learning and I do like physical exercise. I just would prefer to be sucked into my bookcase for the day, whereas my daughter would prefer to move mountains.

Knowing who you are and what gives your life purpose, meaning and satisfaction is essential. It makes life worthwhile. It gives your life colour, depth and direction.

We are meaning-making machines and we operate at our best when our meaning and purpose has clarity, resonance and authenticity.

I'm sure you have met many people who seem so confident,

accomplished and switched on. You have probably wondered how they can exhibit such mastery. You have probably wondered how they know exactly what to do to achieve what they have. I'm sure they started with working on knowing who they are.

So how do we go about knowing ourselves?

'We are like onions', to quote a line from the movie "Shrek".

I'm sure you may have preferred a more attractive analogy than a vegetable that is pungent in taste and makes you cry when handled – or maybe that is how you feel you are going through life at the moment anyway.

I use the onion as an analogy because there are many layers to who we are as well – layers that have been added by time, experiences and obligations. However, there is a core to the onion, just as there is a core to you. We just need to peel back the layers to tap into this. I hope there will not be too many tears in the process!

Knowing your core innate goodness and values is essential because this permeates through all the other layers of your life.

It also gives you something to come back to over and over again as your directional signpost in life – and provides a strong, resilient life foundation.

In this chapter, I elaborate on how to discover your unique personal characteristics so that you can become confident in yourself and your place in the world. This will help you to be an authentic leader who guides and influences from your own special space. I also discuss identifying your shame triggers that will have developed through your western culture socialisation. These triggers may rob you of your belief in yourself unless you understand their influence on you.

Nuture vs. Nature

My grandfather was a business entrepreneur. My mother was too, and I have followed in their footsteps as an accountant and business owner. I also have many, many cousins and second cousins who are accountants. It's too early to know what my daughter's profession will be, but she is an assistant manager in a business at present.

I firmly believe there are biological influences that impact what we do as adults.

You could start your journey of discovery by looking at your family to see if there are any biologically-based traits that you have inherited, which determine what you are currently doing in life.

It may be a fabulous opportunity to document your family history or at least have some in-depth conversations with your family about what makes them tick.

There's much scientific evidence that some 50% of the variations in human personality are associated with genetic factors.

Like many others, I have watched the television show, *Who do you think you are?* with great fascination. It is so interesting to see the genetic traits from different generations flowing through to the people filmed. There was one particularly memorable show that was really intriguing because it seemed that all family members in previous generations were sports-minded, while the subject matter was not. He had to delve more deeply into his family history to find the artist who gave him his genetic characteristics. You could see his genuine relief when he found his artistic ancestor. I believe he must have felt totally out of step with his family until that finding.

Of course, you might be doing what you are doing because it was easy to follow the path created by your parents and/or your family. This is fine, so long as it feels right for you.

How do you know if it is right for you?

The ultimate litmus test is your physical and mental well-being. If you are constantly ill, either physically or mentally, this may indicate some dis-ease with your current situation. It is always best to seek medical help to determine the cause of any chronic health issue.

Certainly, when you are taking positive actions in your life, based on the true core of who you are, there is a sense of contentment, satisfaction and knowing that flows through your day and life. And it just feels good.

Our unique personality

The psychological definition of 'personality', taken from the dictionary, is:

a. the total of the physical, mental, emotional and social characteristics of an individual.
b. the organised pattern of behavioural characteristics of the individual.

There are two traits to your personality – your character and your temperament.

Your character comes from your day-to-day experiences, such as your childhood games; your parents' interests and values; your community's societal norms; what is considered polite, dangerous or exciting; when to laugh, cry, relax. There are many, many cultural forces that build your character and determine your beliefs about how life is meant to be.

Your temperament is the collection of biological-based tendencies that determine your consistent patterns of feeling, thinking and behaving.

As I mentioned earlier, my daughter is an extrovert but I'm an introvert. These traits are part of our individual temperaments.

There are some insightful online tools available now to explore your temperament – your unique identity.

The two that I would recommend to you, which will assist you to understand yourself better, are:

1. Instinctive Drives[5] – www.instinctivedrives.com
2. Character Strengths[6] – www.viame.org

Both reports produced by these online tools are essential, in my view, to help with knowing who you are. They are both relatively inexpensive as well.

Instinctive Drives (ID)
As stated on their website:

Everyone has a natural way of doing things that works best for them. The Instinctive Drives Questionnaire reveals your innate drives and motivations, uncovering exactly what you need to be at your best – both personally and professionally.

We introduced this system into our business a few years ago, on the recommendation of our external Chair of our Board of Directors. We even use it as part of our recruitment process, so we ensure we have the most suitable person for the role that we are wanting to fill.

We know that people work best when they are working true to their natural traits. This creates a win-win situation for our business.

I love solving problems. I know that this is the reason why I am an accountant/financial planner in public practice. I discovered this fact when I became the Financial Controller of a private hospital for 15 months. Once I had solved all the immediate problems in my area that needed to be addressed and moved into the regular every-day/every-month process, I was bored.

The Board of Directors of the hospital was waiting for a new General Manager to commence. They would not allow the Nursing Director and me to explore any other solutions for the wider issues for the hospital, so I became physically ill from the frustration, lack of control and the non-resolution of the problems I could clearly see. I also suffered from anxiety and stress.

I finally resigned and returned to being an accountant in public practice, which was the start of my journey to building my own business in an environment that suited me best.

When I investigated my personal ID, my own report generated by the ID questionnaire, it said – "Problems … who needs them? You do". There are many other amazing insights in my personal I.D. report that assist me to work at my best. I also use it regularly to reflect on who I am and how I am interacting with the world.

In our business, we have used these reports for team building. We have had sessions where we have looked at each other's instinctive drives to understand each other better. This has led to greater respect and appreciation of our differences.

There is also an ID community where you can connect and review how best to approach different people with their different IDs.

I would thoroughly recommend finding out your ID.

I would also thoroughly recommend using this tool when you are building a work team that you are leading.

Character Strengths

The Character Strengths process has grown out of the Positive Psychology movement.

In 1999, Marty Seligman, then President of the American Psychological Association, started looking at a better understanding of what makes a person have a good life.

As a result of a three-year rigorous process, 55 renowned scholars and practitioners came up with the VIA *Classification of Character Strengths and Virtues*. The classification identifies 24 strengths of character that are nested under six higher order categories called virtues.

Character Strengths are the components for a good life. These are the qualities that are valued in ourselves, our friends, our children, our business colleagues and in our leaders.

Everyone has a particular configuration of the 24 strengths – some are overused and some are underused.

As humans, we tend to focus on the negative more so than the positive. It isn't to say that we should forget about the negative; we just don't have to wallow in it. We have a propensity to be hooked into our internal dialogue telling us what is bad about ourselves and therefore take less time looking at the good.

The Character Strengths test will help you to shift the focus from what is wrong to what is strong in you.

Make certain you look at the top strengths before you head to the bottom strengths!

The sense of engagement or flow with your life comes when you are expressing your strengths to achieve a life goal or work task. You feel like everything is right in the world, as well as feeling comfortable in your own skin. This is a wonderful basis to develop self-confidence.

When I went overseas in 2010, I spent a week in Madrid living with a family and honing my Spanish speaking skills. In 2012, I discovered the Character Strengths test and found that one of my top signature strengths is love of learning.

It was such a revelation to me. I had always wondered why I was a course-junkie, always enrolling in new learning. I also had wondered why, whenever I travelled, there needed to be some form of learning as part of the trip.

I am much more aware now of this characteristic, and my propensity to overuse it. I certainly save a lot of money on course fees now! These days, I take lots of time to assess the purpose, need and use of the course before I sign up. This allows me to consider whether I'm just hooked on the learning for learning's sake.

There are many ways you can use the knowledge that you will gain from discovering your Character Strengths.

I would recommend that you purchase the book, *Character Strengths Matter – How to Live a Full Life,* by Shannon Polly and Kathryn Britton.[7] This book will explain how you can apply your own character strengths to your personal, family and business life, and no doubt help you live a good life.

You could organise for your family to do the online questionnaire and use the results in your discussions about family traits.

Your Character Strengths will also be used as a reference in determining your 'why' in the chapter called, 'Know Your Why'.

Who is living your life?

I have discussed here the reasons why it is important to find your core drives, beliefs and traits. I have given you some tools to assist with your journey to finding the real you.

However, we don't live in a vacuum; although, sometimes I wish I did. We have many roles that we fill: I am a mother, friend, and business partner, to name a few. With each of the roles we play, we have very special people who influence our thinking about ourselves and the world.

I would recommend that you look at the people who are in your life and work out how much they may be dictating terms in your life. You may find that you have a veritable committee of people telling you what to feel, how to live your life, what to think and what to do.

Women have traditionally been the carers in the family and sometimes our obligations to the people we care about suppress what we want to do for ourselves. Often there may be no alternative, but it is a worthwhile exercise to look at the role equation in your life.

In Dr Ian Gawler's book, *The Mind that Changes Everything*, there is an exercise on page 49 called 'The exercise for reclaiming your life'.[8] With permission from Dr Gawler, I have set this out below, with some modifications for the context here.

The exercise for reclaiming your life

Take a sheet of A4 paper and turn it on its side. Using a pencil, make a small egg shape in the middle and write 'ME' in it. Now draw pencil lines radiating like spokes to other eggs circling your own. In these outer eggs write the names of the people who live your life with you – parents, children, life partner, business partners, boss, employees, bank manager, mentors, role models, lady over the back fence, etc. You may need a few layers of eggs to fit them all in!

When you have completed the task, take an eraser and determine to make a change. Erase the connecting ties of the people who are dictating terms that are not supporting you and what you want to do in your life. As you physically erase the connecting ties, inwardly thank the people for helping you to date as well, as you symbolically release them.

Hold onto the people that are worth keeping and note what they bring to your life on your sheet of paper.

Dr Gawler has set out another way you can do this

contemplative exercise as follows. You may find this beneficial to break the ties of the people who are living your life for you.

The exercise for unloading your committee
Imagine all the unconstructive, unhelpful people on your particular committee. Gather them together in your mind, then put them on an imaginary bus and take them for a long drive. Put them off the bus! Whoopee! Put a sign up on the front of the bus. No passengers! Leave the committee behind. Start driving your own bus!

In the book, *The Top 5 Regrets of the Dying*, by Bronnie Ware, she identified that the most common regret of all was, "I wish I'd had the courage to live a life true to myself, not the life others expected of me".[9]

Don't be one of these people.

Hopefully, I have given you plenty of personal reasons for knowing who *you* truly are. I will discuss the importance of this in terms of leadership later in this chapter.

Firstly, I want to discuss one other important ingredient for knowing yourself.

The shame web

In the Western world, our social conditioning results in low self-esteem and lack of confidence for many people.

Our basic human desire is to be accepted by our community – our tribe – our mob. This is a fundamental human need. We want to belong.

In Brené Brown's book, *I Thought It Was Just Me (but it isn't)*, she explores the "shame web" that is built from conflicting and competing social-community expectations.

Brené Brown[10] spent years researching shame and the impact on our community. She found that women often feel shame because of what our society has determined to be acceptable and unacceptable for women.

As she says in her book, these expectations dictate:

- *Who we should be.*
- *What we should be.*
- *How we should be.*

There are a lot of 'shoulds' there!

Just think about the amount of images we see of the 'perfect' woman's body. It's funny really, because the waif-like, child-like image that is the norm for Western women is so totally unachievable. Even most of the models who strive to maintain this image have to undergo extreme food deprivation or end up with eating disorders to constantly achieve the desired look for the photo shoots. Then of course there is PhotoShop that can ensure a perfect image every time.

When I was growing up, the model to aspire to be like was Twiggy. Even today Twiggy still has long lanky blonde hair matched by a long lanky body. My heritage is German so my body soon became voluptuous and buxom, and to top it off, I have red curly hair with lots of freckles.

I know I experienced lots of shame during my teenage years because of the standardised and falsified images of so-called beauty, and I have never really accepted my voluptuousness. This led to a life-long struggle with my weight and eating habits.

The sad thing is that if I was born in the 18th or 19th century, my body would have been revered and I would have been sought after by the artists of the time to be captured in their artwork. How ironic is that?

Advances in technology, with the internet and social media, mean that we see more of these beauty images than ever before. It is estimated that today's teenager may be faced with more perfect-body images in a week than their grandmother would have seen in a lifetime.

Adding to that pressure are the images we see in our media depicting how we should be and look as wives and mothers.

We are expected to have perfect homes, cook the perfect meal (to *MasterChef* standards no less) and have the best-behaved, well-dressed children in the neighbourhood – all images that are totally unachievable.

There may be people in your life who you identified in the previous exercise who are very good at bringing up the shame in you.

I have written about shame and shame triggers because it can often be these factors that make us act small. When the shame is rampant, we want to hide, be quiet and in some cases, even disappear.

This book is about leadership and if you want to be a leader and help a group achieve a goal, then you need to be seen, be confident and really, really know who you are and where you are heading.

My experience also is that when there is a power struggle for leadership, shame can be used as a tool to make you go away.

The classic example of shaming happened very publicly in Australia when our first woman Prime Minister, Julia Gillard, (in office 2010–2013) was vilified for being barren (she has no children) and for not having cooked in her kitchen in her home. What relevance these facts had to her ability to lead our country remains a mystery to me.

Thankfully, her speech in Parliament on 9 October 2012 addressing these comments means that it is less likely that this type of verbal attack on a female leader in the public space will happen again. Although you may want to read my caution in Chapter 3, 'Know Your Playing Field', about moral licensing.

When I was the Financial Controller at the private hospital, I also experienced a shaming incident that affected me deeply.

The Nursing Director and I had determined that we needed another humidicrib for the maternity section of the hospital; this section was the most profitable one within the hospital and had the highest occupancy.

I prepared a report for the Directors that included the statistics showing the number of births where a humidicrib was required. It showed that we were hiring humidicribs regularly, and set out the figures proving how profitable this section was and how this purchase would save money for the hospital. The costs/benefit analysis was very detailed.

I presented the report at the Board meeting. The first response I had from one Director was, "Oh! My wife likes to spend money too!".

I looked around the table at these men and realised that I could have shown them that I had invented the cure for cancer and they would not have believed me.

Their unconscious bias had pigeonholed me with 'all' women and assumed that my behaviour would be no different. I will discuss unconscious bias more in the Chapter, 'Know Your Playing Field'.

This Director's reaction certainly shamed me into silence and we did not obtain our humidicrib at that point. It was purchased when the two male managers arrived at the hospital. There were many instances like this one that eventually caused me to leave this job.

Because shame brings up fear – fear of not belonging, fear of being thought to be a fool, fear of not being perfect, fear of failure, fear of not being good enough – it is important to understand what triggers shame in you.

The usual human reactions to fear are that we fight, flight or freeze. It is our automatic biological response.

In most cases, women will normally adopt the flight or freeze (silent) response. Certainly, this was my reaction in the example that I gave. I was shamed into silence and did not continue with my presentation about the humidity crib.

Shame resilience

In her book, *I Thought It Was Just Me (but it isn't)*, Brené Brown has identified four steps to shame resilience. I have summarised these in my own words below.

1. Recognise your shame triggers.
2. Practise critical awareness through your shame responses.

3. Reach out to your support network.
4. Speak shame to express what you feel and ask for what you need so that you don't have to feel as ashamed again.

Recognise your shame triggers

Shame is a highly-individualised experience, and there are no universal shame triggers. Some of the categories that affect women are appearance and body image, motherhood, family, parenting, money and work, mental and physical health, sex, aging, being stereotyped and labelled, speaking out and surviving trauma. Yes, it is a long list. You may have some of these or none. I recommend you take some time to consider your reaction to each one of these shame triggers.

These are all identified by Brown as 'unwanted identities'. On the list is speaking out, which comes with the leadership territory. Ambitious women are seen as loud and pushy; although, ambitious men are seen as competitive and assertive.

Recognising your shame triggers may make you feel vulnerable and weak. Certainly, when you are feeling shame you feel overwhelmed with confusion, fear and judgement. Strangely once you can identify your shame triggers and find the words around these, their power diminishes. This ties in with my later discussions about the neuroscience on managing emotions – refer to Chapter 4, 'Know Your Tipping Point'.

It doesn't mean you are not going to arc up when someone criticises your child because you feel shame about your parenting. It just means that you are aware that it is happening and hopefully you can manage an appropriate response, rather than wanting to rip the other person's head from their body – figuratively, of course. This comment tells you how I usually react to shame. I step in and want to fight. It's not always the best response when you are negotiating!

Practise critical awareness through your shame responses

Shame works like the zoom lens on a camera. You feel like you are a kangaroo in the headlights. You are alone and struggling with this feeling of not being good enough. The reality is that we all feel shame. When you step back and realise that other people are experiencing the same, the power of shame is lessened.

Reach out to your support network

When the feeling of not being good enough happens, you just want to run away and hide. Silence feeds shame. When you reach out to your support network and speak about it, the power of the emotion is lessened. You often realise the people in your support network have had similar experiences. It normalises your situation. In Chapter 4, 'Know your Tipping Point' I have discussed having venting partners and the benefit of this support.

Speak shame to express what you feel and ask for what you need so that you don't have to feel as ashamed again

Finding the words about the emotions we are feeling is a powerful tool for diffusing the effects of emotions, and certainly shame.

Another technique for dealing with shame or any other strong emotion is self-compassion. This is where you extend compassion to yourself when you are feeling inadequate, a failure, or any other general suffering.

Kristin Neff has identified three main components of

self-compassion – self-kindness, realising your common humanity (everyone experiences shame and strong emotions) and mindfulness. I discuss the benefits of mindfulness in Chapter 11, 'Nourishment and Replenishment'.

Brené Brown has three follow up books that I recommend you should also read. These are:

- *The Gifts of Imperfection*
- *Daring Greatly*
- *Rising Strong*

Knowing yourself and leadership

Leadership is about *helping or enabling others to reach a common goal or solve a mutual problem.*

Leadership is about guiding and inspiring. Of course, to enable this to happen effectively, you must have some form of influence. Sometimes the influence will come from formal authority because you are the boss. In most cases, though, it will need to come from earned authority.

In fact, it is common for a person with no formal authority but with earned authority to have more influence because they have earned the respect, trust and allegiance of those who work with others. I'm sure you know people that fit this bill.

There is no reason why you cannot be the same.

Certainly, when you know who you are and how you react to the world, you have more confidence in yourself. This means you can make effective decisions that make things happen, which in turn leads to influencing those around you to accept and do what needs to happen.

Authenticity in leadership is valued today.

Summary

- Knowing who you are and what makes you unique is essential to life and leadership. This is the starting point of discovering what gives your life meaning and purpose. Learning what makes you strong, not wrong, feeds self-confidence. When you are confident and living according to your unique talents, you are more able to step up and lead people.
- Take some time to see who is living your life for you. There may be a committee of people telling you what to feel, how to live your life, and judging how you are thinking and being. Be prepared to ask this committee to leave you alone so you can determine your own destiny.
- Take some time to identify your shame triggers too. These 'unwanted identities' can make you feel vulnerable and alone, and not good enough. Find the methods to mitigate your shame responses so that your self-confidence can shine through. This will include self-compassion, venting partners, and finding your words about shame.
- When you know yourself and how you react to the world, you have more confidence in yourself. You can then step out in the world to influence and guide others. This is all part of authentic leadership.

CHAPTER TWO

KNOW YOUR WHY

"He who has a why to live for, can bear almost any how."
Nietzsche

Martin Luther King Jr., was killed 4 April 1968, in Memphis, Tennessee. During his life, his 'why' meant that he could bear almost any 'how'. His 'why' was built around his overwhelming desire to achieve freedom from racial hatred for all.

His speech, 'I Have A Dream', where he clearly expressed his "why" straight from the heart, is immortalised as one of the truly inspirational speeches of all time.

King endured watching people brutalised and killed for the sake of this joint cause. He also made the ultimate sacrifice with his own life.

There are many examples throughout history of people who have clearly known why they existed and chose to make unimaginable sacrifices for necessary changes in our world. Martin Luther King Jr's story may seem too aspirational for you, and that may be true. I simply want to demonstrate the power of his 'why' with his story.

I also believe there is a parallel between King's cause against racial hatred and our cause for women's fair representation in the power decisions of the world. Each cause requires a struggle for change of a status quo that has been in place for a very long time.

Leaders and organisations that are good at communicating their belief, draw us to them. We feel like we belong and are safe, special and important. This then allows us to find our 'why' and become inspired.

So our 'why' ripples out into the world as well as ripples inwards to ground us and provide the basis for 'what' we do and 'how' we do it. Simon Sinek explains this process in his book, *Start with Why – How Great Leaders Inspire Everyone to Take Action*.

As he says, this is how our brains work as well. The limbic part of our brain, based at the centre of our brain, is the powerhouse for all our emotions. This is where all our human behaviour stems from and decision-making is done. There is no capacity for language in this ancient part of the brain.

Our newest area of our brain, based in the outer part of our brain, is the neocortex. This is the *Homo sapien* brain and is where all our analytical thoughts and language come from. This area of the brain justifies the emotional decisions we have made in the limbic part of our brain.

I'm sure you have experienced many situations where you have said, "It just feels right". You may even then have found the language to justify the reason for the decision.

This chapter looks more closely at the power of having a strong 'why' for everything you do, including special projects and leadership activities. I also provide a framework for discovering your own unique 'why'.

How to discover your 'why'

We first start with the work you have done in the previous chapter. In particular, we are looking at the factors that determine your temperament, because temperament is the collection of biological-based tendencies that determine your emotional patterns of feeling, thinking and behaving. Remember, emotional patterns are the markers for your limbic brain.

Discovering your temperament is not an easy process and may take lots of time as you experiment with, and identify, how you react in your world.

My recommendation for this process is as follows:

1. If you aren't already using a journal for writing, I recommend that you start now as part of learning your 'why'. Make it a special process too. Go to the stationery shop and celebrate by purchasing something special to write in, and even buy some special pens to write with. I have been writing in a journal for years and it is so cathartic on so many levels.

2. Study your top character strengths that were determined by the online 'Character Strengths' questionnaire. Take each signature strength and think about how each of these strengths has played a role in your life successes. Think about what effect these signature strengths have on you and others in your day-to-day living.

   Write down your thoughts from in your journal as you do this exercise. Don't worry too much about the words you are writing – just write. This isn't going to be marked or assessed by anyone other than you.

Try to capture the emotions you feel and translate them into words that resonate with you.

You could try drawing your thoughts and emotions. You could even do a mind map. Dot points are good if you are struggling. Try to articulate what you are feeling and thinking.

3. Pick one of your top character strengths and observe during a day or week how you use the strength throughout your daily routine, and especially in your interactions with your life partner, children, friends, work colleagues and even the peripheral people during the day, e.g. the person making the coffee; the check-out person at the supermarket. Observe how you feel when you are using this strength.

4. Each evening spend 10–15 minutes with your journal and write down your observations from Exercise 3, especially around how you felt using these character strengths.

Again, remember to just let the words flow. Don't worry about the rules of language – grammar, spelling etc. Remember, dot points are good if you are struggling.

Try to capture the emotions you felt and translate them into words that resonate with you. Draw, mind map – whatever allows you to capture and appreciate who you are when you are feeling at your best and in tune with the world.

5. Each week take some time to reflect on Exercise 2 and 4. Find the words that seem to be consistent in your writing, or drawing, or mind mapping etc.

6. Start to write some sentences around why you want to live a certain way, and what values are important to you in your daily life. Really explore this and find lots of rich words that capture your emotions and inspire you to be who you are.

7. Practise expressing these ideas with your close friends and colleagues. You will find that as you start to say the words out loud, there will be a different resonance to you. You may find that you need to explore other words or add more descriptive adjectives.

8. Each morning start the day by visualising yourself carrying these words and/or sentences with you, and take time during the day to become aware of how you feel being the person you are with these words and/or sentences as your guiding force.

9. Regularly revisit this exercise, especially when life events happen that distract or disrupt your rhythm. It is very cathartic to write in your journal about these events. At the same time, you can revisit your signature strengths and maybe revisit the words you are using for your sentence. Writing in a journal is a fabulous tool for helping you through the tough times as well as the exciting times, especially if you write from the perspective of what is strong not wrong.

What we want to achieve with this exploration is a 'Life Sentence' (no, this is not a jail term) that you can use as your blueprint for everything you do in life. In business, these are called mission statements. I like to use the term Life Sentence or Personal Value Proposition (PVP) for my personal journey.

Again, I would thoroughly recommend that you acquire the book, *Character Strengths Matter – How to Live a Full Life*, by Shannon Polly and Kathryn Britton. There are many sections and exercises in this book that will help you with your exploration process.

Don't forget your lesser strengths – explore these too.

This is your journey, and like any journey you start where you are and take the first steps slowly and carefully until you find the path to follow. Just make certain you keep going. Also remember to stop and reflect so that you can savour where you have been. The journal you have kept will help with this. You could look at the Basic Steps I have set out in Chapter 5, and use this process for discovering your 'why'.

Your 'why' in practice

Can you imagine how essential Martin Luther King Jr's 'why' would have been to every decision, action and process that he undertook in his life?

This is how powerful your Life Sentence – PVP can be in motivating you to live the life you want. It will determine how you will 'be' each day and what you choose to do. Your goals will be meaningful and you will bring the best qualities of yourself to every part of your life and your relationships.

My Life Sentence – PVP (after many years of soul searching) is:

I touch the lives of everyone I meet with compassion, under-standing and generosity of spirit, and I work constantly and joyfully towards a world full of peace, justice and fairness.

I also have a short version – "I want to help make the world fairer, kinder and more joyful."

Because of my Life Sentence – PVP, I have pursued learning around compassion, communication, emotional intelligence, world justice, peace, and so on.

To understand joy, I became a Laughter Wellness profes-sional and include Laughter Yoga in my weekly mental and physical health practices.

I know that I am at my most compassionate and understand-ing when I am physically, mentally and emotionally fit, so I have a regular exercise regime as well as a good eating plan. I medi-tate most days to become more mindful and understanding, so that I am calm and confident. Notice I said "most days" for the meditation practice.

It is very easy to be distracted by the daily noise coming from all forms of media to which we are exposed. I am no different. Having my Life Sentence – PVP though means that I can pull myself away from distractions more easily than I could in the past.

When I am considering a course of action in life, I ask myself where that action is going to fit in my Life Sentence – PVP. This certainly has slowed my habit of investing in study programs just for the sake of it: I now choose more wisely.

Whenever I am establishing my next goals in life, I ask myself where that goal will fit with my Life Sentence – PVP.

This book is actually a product of my Life Sentence – PVP, and it is part of my quest to help create a fairer world for everyone.

All great leaders have a clear 'why', so spend the time you need to discover yours. Treasure it and communicate it often.

Be the sun in your universe

The sun is the star at the centre of our solar system and is responsible for the earth's climate and weather. It provides our light and warmth during the day as it shines down upon us. I encourage you to see yourself in the same way for your own personal universe – your family, your friends, the people you are leading.

As caregivers, there can be a tendency to be available to give support for as many people as we can, often to the detriment of ourselves. We also sometimes look outwards and seek replenishment in the external world, not realising that our source of power and wisdom is within.

Imagine our world if the sun lost power. It would be a very dark, dismal and cold place to live.

If your power diminished, what would be the impact on your universe? I'm sure there would be many, many people who would be bereft because of the loss of your warmth, light and energy.

I'm hoping that this analogy will allow you to see that your power and strength are paramount. Yes, allow your warmth and light to shine as far and as wide as you can, but not at the expense of extinguishing your own personal power.

The message in this analogy is very important to your life and leadership journey. Leadership requires much collaboration, and you will need to find ways of protecting yourself from unreasonable demands from others. This is not a selfish act. This is a brave act for the benefit of everyone in your universe.

Summary

- Every life and leadership project needs a 'why' because it ripples out into the world as well as inwards to ground us, and it provides the basis for how we are and what we do.
- Complete the exercise to discover your personal 'why', which will lead to your own Life Sentence or Personal Value Proposition – PVP.
- Your Life Sentence – PVP will form the basis for everything you do in life, including the leadership projects you choose. Keep it treasured and communicate it often, especially to your close network.
- Be the sun in your universe. Understand that you are the centre of your universe and be brave to protect your power so that it remains strong. This will ensure that your light, warmth and energy shine far and wide without losing power.

CHAPTER THREE

KNOW YOUR PLAYING FIELD

> "Don't fake it until you make it. Fake it until you become it."
> Amy Cuddy

As women leaders, you need to be aware of the arena into which you are striding. In this chapter, I explore some of the human traits that may change the nature of the playing field in which you are participating. Hopefully this will allow you to negotiate some of the traps, pitfalls, and barriers that exist not only on the playing field but also within you.

As humans, emotions are powerful motivators of our behaviour. We like to believe that we are rational creatures because of our conscious awareness. However, we are biological beings so emotions, not rational thought, drive our behaviour. Whom to marry, where to live, or even what we select for dinner, are decisions we make not by reason, but rather, according to how we feel.

We have emotions because we need them. Our minds are taking in and assessing internal and external information gathered via our senses, constantly sifting through data looking out for danger in order to keep us safe. Most of this information processing operates below the level of consciousness, in the subconscious. If we were aware of all of it, we would be totally overwhelmed and would not be able to function.

When faced with very complex situations, it is our deep subconscious brain – our threat detector, our limbic system – not only our cerebral cortex – that most often moves us to action. Especially when our fundamental wellbeing is at stake.

I have endeavoured to cover some of the major human traits that may impact your journey as a woman leader in this chapter. I believe that the first step for change is awareness. We only know what we know at any one point in time. Once awareness happens, you can begin learning different processes to influence who you are, and those around you.

Armed with this learning, as Amy Cuddy said, "You can fake it until you become it".

Unconscious bias

I remember the day that Bridget came to our school. I was in Grade 6 at the State School in Barcaldine, a small town in outback Queensland. Actually, if you stuck a pin into the centre of the map of Queensland, you would be pretty close to finding it.

Bridget was different. She had come from the 'big smoke' – the city. Bridget was a carrot top with long bright orange hair and lots and lots of freckles everywhere. She really stood out from us.

Bridget was also extremely smart, so nobody wanted to play with her.

This stand-off went on for a number of weeks, until one day I decided that I would approach her and see if we could include her in our play group.

This was the start of one of the best friendships of my life. We just clicked. I vividly remember that wonderful feeling of being with a kindred spirit that makes life special and warms the heart. These connections are precious.

This moment in my history could have had a different outcome if I'd have chosen to follow my unconscious bias of non-acceptance of Bridget because she did not fit into my concept of normal. It may have been that I started taunting her and highlighting her differences to everyone around me. This could have so easily ended as a school bullying incident. Fortunately, it did not.

I raise the issue of unconscious bias because this has a major impact in our playing fields within business and government. It is one of the most important influencing factors to be aware of, if you are a leader or want to be a leader. Unconscious bias is also one of the major contributing factors to our unfair playing fields.

Unconscious bias is part of being human. It comes from our learning of the world and how we process information. Bridget came from the city. She looked very different from anyone I had encountered before. Therefore, in my mind, I was not going to include her in my everyday processes.

Biases help us to use previous knowledge to inform new decisions. It's a kind of cognitive shorthand. We are not programmed with enough cognitive resources to make every decision with a fresh mind.

Imagine the chaos in the morning, preparing to go to work, if you had to assess whether everything on your breakfast plate was safe to eat or not. Mmm – egg on toast – I wonder if the chicken that laid this egg is healthy. Am I going to die from salmonella poisoning? Should I eat this egg or not?

No, my decision process in the morning is – I bought these eggs at the supermarket and there is a use-by date on the carton. I can assume that it is pretty safe for me to eat the egg on my toast.

When we are looking at the playing fields in workplaces, unconscious bias means women can struggle to be included in the levels of influence, as they are often not seen as leaders.

Our society has been traditionally structured where men occupy the public space and women occupy the private space. This has created the societal norm that men occupy the positions of influence. Perception is everything.

In a paper released by UN Women – National Committee Australia in May 2015, entitled 'Rethinking merit – Why the meritocracy is failing Australian businesses',[11] other reasons identified for the lack of a level playing field for women were:

- *They remain responsible for the majority of unpaid care work in Australia.*
- *They are less likely to be offered formal training and development.*
- *They are often excluded from the informal networking, which later leads to opportunities arising for men.*

Here are other examples of how the playing field is unfair:

In 2012, Yale undertook a study about recruitment for a student applying for a lab manager position. Half the scientists were given the application with a male name attached, and half were given identical applications with a female name attached. Results found that the 'female' applicants were rated significantly lower than the 'males' in competence and hire-ability. The scientists also offered lower starting salaries to the 'female' applicants – 14 per cent less than the 'male' applicants.

The really significant part of this study was that the scientists taking part in the recruitment exercise were both male and female.

A recent study of financial and other rewards given by businesses who view their practices to be designed around merit, found that larger monetary rewards were given to male managers than female managers. This phenomenon has been dubbed the 'merit paradox'. Isn't that strange? A focus on merit results in more biased outcomes.

This unfair playing field is where you will be playing as a leader. It will be a source of immense frustration until change happens. I know that it has been one of the greatest frustrations for me in my career, and it was the main reason why I became self-employed and built my own business.

Unconscious bias permeates all of us.

In the words of Yassmin Abdel-Magied, founder of Youth Without Borders, "Unconscious bias is not an accusation rather bias is something that needs to be identified, acknowledged and mitigated against so that the circumstances of your birth do not dictate your future."

There is some amazing research available now that I'm hopeful will speed up the change.

The Neuroleadership Institute published in their May 2014 journal an article called 'Breaking Bias'.[12] They also developed business programs to assist with the mitigation of all 150 cognitive biases that we humans have.

There is more information on this research in the section 'Bias Busting' in Chapter 6, 'Basic Skills Required'.

Some steps that you can take to mitigate the unfairness of the playing field because of unconscious bias are as follows:

1. Be aware of how you act. See the situations where you turn away from someone because they are different from you. Become aware of when you exclude someone from participating because they are different. Observe the people that you include in your playing field. When you can see your own reactions in these situations, you are more likely to make changes to your life and ask for change around you.

2. Understand that unconscious bias exists because we are human. It's not about motivation. It's about biology.

3. Be prepared to ask for extra support, mentoring and understanding because the playing field is not even for women.

4. Demand that there are processes in organisations that address unconscious bias.

5. Demand that biased comments and views are not tolerated.

Moral licensing

As another view of the challenge that women face in a patri-
archal society, I recommend that you listen to the podcast by
Malcolm Gladwell titled 'Episode 1: The Lady Vanishes'. Malcolm
Gladwell's podcasts are available on the website, 'Revisionist
History'.[13]

Gladwell looks at little-known female artist Elizabeth
Thompson Butler, who was nearly the first woman to be voted as
a member of the British Royal Academy of Art in 1879. He looks
at this historic event to discuss the concept of moral licensing
and the discrimination of women.

Moral licensing is the behaviour that you exhibit when you
give yourself permission to do something 'bad' because you've
been 'good'. The classic self-sabotaging example is to do with
dieting – "I've been to the gym and done a work out so I deserve
an ice cream with my dinner".

Researchers have found that this psychological behaviour
may also apply to discrimination. Because USA has voted a
black person as President, this may mean that many people consider that they deserve to be more discriminatory to all black
people. The research is not conclusive though.

However, it is interesting to listen to Gladwell's analysis of the
treatment of Julia Gillard, Australia's first female Prime Minister,
and the discriminatory comments that were made about her as a
woman. He believes that this is a classic example of moral licensing. She was allowed into a position of influence, so some people
believed that it was fine to discriminate against her while she
was in that role, based on gender stereotype.

You may think that other women pioneers have made it easier for you and that you will not receive the same treatment. Gladwell would argue that this is not the case.

I raise this issue so that you do not assume that just because there are more women in senior positions, society's view of women has changed. You may still find resistance and stereotyping around you, and some of it will come from other women.

Combining your caring roles with your leadership role

I never thought I would be a mother. In my 20s, I loved being a career person. Sometime in my early 30s, the biological clock started ticking extremely loudly in my ear and I wanted so much to be a mother.

Of course, nobody told me that just because you want to be a mum, it will necessarily happen. It looked like we were not going to have any children. Because I was an older woman, married to an older man, the chance of conception had been significantly reduced and I had had some physical problems with the mechanics, which impaired the process somewhat as well.

After much heartache, I resigned myself to being a career person again, and then *whamo*, along came our daughter when I was almost 38.

My life had dramatically changed by this time. I was now running my own business as a sole owner, as my first business partner had died the year before. I was really struggling to come to terms with his passing and the impact that had on the business, as well as trying to understand everything that needed to happen to hold the business together.

When you become a mother it is like entering a whole new paradigm. There is no way anyone can prepare you for this either. Yes, people will tell you that everything changes; however, until you experience it the words are hollow.

Neuroscientists are now studying what happens to a woman as a result of pregnancy, and they are discovering that there are significant changes in a new mother's brain, which explain why they become anxious and emotional.

The flood of hormones that happen during pregnancy and just after the birth of the baby, help attract and attach a new mother to her baby. The maternal feelings of overwhelming love, fierce protectiveness and constant worry begin with reactions in the brain.

The greatest brain changes occur with a mother's first child and neurologists are not sure if their brains ever go back to what they were like before childbirth.

Oxytocin is the bonding hormone. This hormone connects us as humans. Women experience a dramatic increase of this hormone during pregnancy, when the baby is born, as well as during child care. Oxytocin also increases as women look at their babies, or hear their babies' sounds and cries, and especially when they snuggle with their babies.

Scientists are also showing that there are similar brain changes for men when they are deeply involved in the caregiving of their children. There was an article published in the *PNAS* Journal of 8 July 2014, titled 'Father's brain is sensitive to childcare experiences', by Abraham, Hendler, Shapira-Lichter, Kanant-Maymom, Zagoory-Sharon and Feldman.[14]

The research showed that a mother's brain was different, though, because they are primed for mothering, with a part of the brain evolved for an automatic response. Men's neural pathways are established with adaptation to the parental role and come with practice, attunement and day-by-day caregiving.

James shared with me as part of his interview for this book that although he has a significant role in the caregiving for his son, he observed that the caring role was much more intense for his wife. Like many couples today, they both work and share the care of their children. They both have careers that are important to them. I found this very insightful of James to have observed this about his wife.

My ex-husband was the primary caregiver for our daughter and I remember him saying to me at one point that he couldn't understand how women could do the caregiving role full-time because it was so demanding.

As more men are involved in caring for their children, they will appreciate what an important role it is, and also how demanding it is. Hopefully, like James, they will also come to appreciate, understand and empathise with what happens to their partners as they deal with the intensity of being a mother.

Understanding is the key to dealing with this dilemma of combining caring and leadership.

Understanding that this is your playing field once you become a mother.

Understanding that you may well experience incredible emotional and physical changes that will overwhelm.

The challenge is that if you are in a position of leadership you need to find ways to compartmentalise your life. Well, this is what I found worked for me.

I tried working from home in the early stages of my daughter's life. We even built a home office specifically for this. However I found I was not present for her when she needed me, and I wasn't present for my business when it needed me either. I had to separate the two roles.

I went back to my business office for work and came home to my family afterwards. This allowed me to separate who I was in my different roles. I found that I could devote my home time to my family and my work time to my business.

Of course, nothing happens in a straight line and there were many times when these boxes overlapped, especially when my daughter or husband was unwell or there were other crises that needed to be dealt with. It was equally true for my business. Sometimes I just needed to immerse myself in the management of the business to keep it on track.

Some of my fondest memories with my daughter were when we were both unwell. I know that sounds perverse. We had the opportunity to snuggle up in bed and get well together. As we healed, there was lots of time to talk and have fun together. It was also a time of putting the rest of the world on hold for a bit.

The other challenge with juggling career and motherhood is to turn down the noise. You will find that there are lots of people who will have opinions about what you are doing and how your family is travelling. Often the strongest critics are the ones closest to you as well. Remember, parenting is a very strong shame trigger for women.

You will also experience guilt that your choices have somehow impacted your child and your family. A lot of this guilt is
exacerbated by the brain changes that I mentioned earlier. There
is this constant underlying worry that pervades every part of
your life. You think your child will grow up scarred because of
your choices.

The reality is that children experience many different situations that could scar them, and you have absolutely no control
over all of them – and may even be unaware of some of them.

In secondary school my daughter was discriminated against
by a teacher. I can assure you this was totally unexpected to me
as a mother, and it was extremely difficult to live through. It was
unexpected because I thought I had found a safe school environment for my child.

This event had lots of ramifications for our family, but we
lived through it. Even my daughter would say that she is stronger
and more resilient because of this experience. Of course, you
wish it didn't happen, but it did.

My approach to dealing with the noise was to focus on my
'why' (Chapter 2), and try to turn down the volume. You will not
always achieve this because there will always be the odd comment
or situation that will just get under your guard. When this happens, just breathe deep and use my next technique, which is to be
in tune with your family. Simply ask yourself these questions:

- Do my children and life partner look healthy and happy?
- Do my children have lots of good connections at school
  and outside school?
- Are my children having fun learning about life?

There are lots of expectations on parents and children to meet educational and life standards. These expectations can often interfere with just having a good life. There is a happy equilibrium for all tensions.

Just determine what is most important for your family and block out the rest of the noise. Life is hopefully a long journey with many learning experiences – some good and some not so good. It's more important to know how to survive and thrive with whatever life throws at you.

In his book, 'The Third Space – Using life's little transitions to find balance and happiness',[15] Dr Adam Fraser has written about the micro-transitions from one role, environment and task to another. Fraser discusses using the gap between the First Space (the role/environment/task where you currently are) and the Second Space (the role/environment/task that you are moving to). He argues that if we take the time to be aware of the Third Space (the gap between the First Space and the Second Space) we will have a more balanced and happy experience in the Second Space – the role, environment and task where we have moved. I would recommend that you read this book. I have set out the basic ideas from the book in Chapter 6, 'Basic Skills Required'.

As women, we are responsible for much of the unpaid care work required in a family, and this often can include the care of elderly parents as well. It just seems to be expected that we will also take responsibility for this caring role. Of course, it will more than likely be what you want to do as well.

As an only daughter I was very close to my mother. When I found out that she was dying from cancer in 1980, I didn't hesitate to put my career on hold and go home to care for her. It was important for me and it was definitely important for my mother for me to be there.

It was only while writing this book that I realised how societal expectations impacted both my brother Jeff and I at that time. Jeff came home as well to be with our mother. His employer accommodated his wish and ensured that his career continued while he was at home taking on this caring role. However, my employer at that time never even considered doing this for me. There was no offer or discussion about how I was going to maintain my career. And I did not think to ask either.

Admittedly we didn't have the technology that we have today that would have made this process easier for me. Still, my brother's employer found ways of ensuring that he continued working, so it was possible.

My time spent caring for my mother lasted for about a year, which was not a lot of time to disrupt my career. However, others may be required to give years and years of devotion. If this happens, it will be a challenge to combine all demands on you. Ask your employer about flexible ways to accommodate this.

I believe it is essential that you consider what is most important to you. I share here a story written by Hazel. When I was interviewing her, I was so touched by her story that I asked her to write it for me. She has kindly done that.

Looking back over my career in Financial Services and reflecting on the way I worked, I can acknowledge the price I paid, particularly as a female. I think the most poignant example of this was during my father's illness. At the time, I was in a senior management role and felt very responsible for my team and the State's results. There was a lot of pressure from above, in relation to reaching targets in what was a very difficult financial market. It was pressure that I wanted to protect the team from, as I believed it was my responsibility to shoulder this.

So this was the background I was dealing with when my 88-year-old Dad took sick. He was admitted to hospital for a series of tests to establish why he had become short of breath – this had happened quickly as the week before he was still playing tennis and swimming every day.

Surprisingly, within a few days Dad's results came back, which confirmed that he had cancer and so treatment was commenced. Even more surprisingly, Dad started to go downhill, which was contrary to the prognosis we had been given and it was put down to the fact that his body was adjusting to the treatment.

The hospital Dad went into was located approximately 30kms from the office, up the freeway. It was a journey that took anywhere between 20 minutes and one hour, depending on the time of day. (If I was in a hurry it always took longer!) My dilemma was – where do I spend my time and how do I balance my responsibilities? I clearly remember feeling guilty when I wasn't with Dad and vice versa. The way I managed this was to drive back and forth to the hospital three times a day.

I know now that managing the situation this way meant that I was never really present in either environment. So the question was always there for me as to what else I could do. I certainly wouldn't have experienced any support had I applied for compassionate leave, and anyway at this stage none of us realised in our wildest imagination just how quickly Dad would deteriorate.

We were all stunned by the fact that the day after his brother had arrived from the UK (and we had a party in the hospital room to celebrate), Dad went into a coma and died the day after that. Even the doctors were taken by surprise.

It was then necessary for me to arrange the funeral and support my mum, as she faced being alone for the first time in her life, and a future without her partner of 65 years. That was when I finally felt it was acceptable to take my two weeks compassionate leave.

The reason that I share this is to highlight the dilemma we as women often feel in our endeavour to balance career with being a partner, mother, sister, or importantly in this case, daughter. If I had my time again I would certainly put everything else on hold for my Dad, because at the end of the day any organisation that can't operate effectively for a few weeks without its key people is operating a poor business model. And, in fact the more we encourage our people to take time out for the things that really matter (family), ultimately the loyalty and commitment I've seen then demonstrated more than compensates for this support.

What I also know now is that it is really impossible to chase the goal of balance, if we view this from the perspective of being equal – let's strive instead for harmony, investing our time in the most important aspects of our life first, in the knowledge that the emphasis will change from time to time and our priorities with it.

Let's empower, support and encourage those around us

to do the same – see this as a strength that good people have, which stems from healthy values. So, ask yourself the question "what really matters to me?" and make sure the answer includes time for those you love.

And finally, wherever you choose to invest your time, truly be there ... without guilt or regret – say "yes" to those you love, and trust that the rest will take care of itself. ☺

Hazel has succinctly identified the issues that we face as primary caregivers.

It is important to work out what is essential and design your life around this need. It is also important to know what works for you around your own, your family's and your career's rhythm.

It is important to ask those that support you to support you through the process.

As Hazel has said too, be present for those that are important. This time is precious.

When I interviewed Jessica for the book and asked her how she combines motherhood and her career, her answer was "unashamedly". I really like that word.

We need to unashamedly demand support from our employers, life partners and anyone who is close to us so that we can combine our careers and our caring roles.

Hormones

We are biological creatures. I keep coming back to this point because, in my experience, we tend to overlook this factor. Our consciousness and our constant thinking cause us to forget that our bodies dictate as well. We believe that our thoughts are who we are.

As women, we are very aware of biological rhythms. Our reproductive cycle has its way of reminding us frequently. Then when our reproductive years are at an end, we have the joy of menopause.

My point for raising this matter in a leadership book is that it is important to physically look after yourself around these amazingly, wonderful and important cycles. I discovered that if I neglected my physical exercise, appropriate eating and good rest time, I paid the price. This is true in terms of overall fitness of course, but in my experience it's doubly important for women leaders.

In the 'NeuroLeadership Journal' of March 2015, there is an article entitled, 'An Ideal Hormone Profile for Leadership: Can you Help Yourself be a Better Leader?' by Josh Davis and Pranjal H. Mehta.[16]

To quote from this journal:

Social neuroendocrinology – the study of hormone systems in social contexts – is showing
(a) that there might be an optimal hormonal profile for leader-ship and
(b) that a person can influence his or her own hormonal pro-file in the short and long term.
   These findings hold across gender, type of organisations (e.g. sports teams, business), and types of leadership challenges (e.g. negotiation, competition, cooperation).

Research suggests that the ideal hormone profile for leadership is high testosterone, low cortisol and context-appropriate oxytocin. Also, the effects of this combination on leadership do not seem to differ for men and women.

Although women have 1/6th the levels of testosterone as men, the impact lies with the fluctuation of this hormone around baseline levels. A high-testosterone/low-cortisol profile has as much benefit to a female leader as a male leader.

The combination of high testosterone and low cortisol appears to be the best mix, resulting in accorded high status as well as being seen as resilient and flexible rather than reactive and confrontational. Someone with a combination of high testosterone and high cortisol could have a tendency to be aggressively over-reactive.

Oxytocin is the bonding hormone, as discussed earlier. Although research is not conclusive, there is speculation that oxytocin may play a role with the social side of leadership.

Leadership is about guiding, inspiring, developing and protecting those in organisations, and these attributes require a large amount of social understanding. A leader often needs to listen attentively and empathise non-judgementally before making decisions that are necessary for the group or organisation.

It is thought that oxytocin may assist with this socialisation.

Unfortunately, there is no evidence that women have an advantage because of the caring roles that we undertake, and oxytocin is not exclusive to females. In fact, high oxytocin in the wrong circumstances can lead to inappropriately high trust of others.

The NeuroLeadership Journal also provides guidance on how to change hormone levels to assist with the leadership process. The journal discusses four features of the neuroendocrine system that a leader can leverage:

1. Hormone-behaviour relationships go both ways. A leader's hormone profile influences leadership behaviour but simultaneously the leadership behaviour influences a leader's hormone profile. Perceiving your status as a leader can increase testosterone levels.

2. Hormones are relatively slow-acting; however, because we are biological creatures, once we get a biochemical process going then momentum happens. A small increase of testosterone leads to change in behaviour, which leads to the release of more testosterone, leading to an upward spiral.

3. Our actions can change our hormone levels. Amy Cuddy, in her TED Talk, 'Body Language Shapes Who You Are',[17] talks about the power poses that can be used to increase testosterone but lower cortisol. The power stand is standing tall, chest and arms expanded, hands on hips and wide stance. This is basically the Wonder Woman stance.

4. Looking after our health – diet and sleep – also helps to keep our cortisol levels low. Sometimes good sleep is not always possible when you are a parent. At these times, you may need to be super-aware that your leadership skills are not at their peak. You may need to delay important decisions or meetings (where possible) until you are physically stronger.

Oxytocin has been known to increase with a 15-minute massage or social support. Having a coffee with a friend or mentor will help increase oxytocin, which lowers cortisol. This may assist when there is a stressful meeting planned.

How you think about a situation can change your hormone mix. Testosterone levels go up when a person is anticipating competition or status challenge. This can often happen on a project when resources may need to be shared across groups or approval is to be granted for one group over the other. Scarcity and vigilance create stressful threat-focused situations. Cortisol levels will be higher. It may make collaboration challenging. A leader will need to be aware of these situations and try to alter the mindset of the group to ensure the best decisions are made.

High cortisol levels also may result in excessive rumination about a situation that is then taken home and stewed over long into the night.

Mindfulness training has been shown to decrease cortisol levels. Becoming aware of the emotions and thought patterns, and reframing the situation can lead to lower cortisol. When we have a cool head, it allows for better collaboration or negotiation and hopefully better outcomes.

There is more guidance in Chapter 11, 'Nourishment and Replenishment'.

Summary

- Our behaviour is largely motivated by emotions deep in our subconscious threat-detecting circuitry. As a woman leader, you will need to be very aware of the human nuances that will govern your behaviour and the people around you.

- Unconscious bias and moral licensing may impact your journey to become a leader, as well as colour your leadership experience. It is important to be aware of these human traits so that you can navigate the pitfalls, traps and barriers that arise.
- Combining your caring and leadership roles is challenging. Being a mother heightens the emotions you are going to feel. Having any caring role will do the same. These experiences are extremely important for your life's journey so you do not want to forego them. However, this means as a leader you will need to look after yourself. Ask for support as much as possible, and turn down the noise of expectation around you.
- We are biological creatures. Our mind and body play an important part in how we feel. As women leaders, it is doubly important to be aware of your hormone make-up and take care of yourself physically. I have provided some wonderful information from neuroscience that will help you stay physically strong and influence the important hormones that ensure you are an effective leader.

CHAPTER FOUR

KNOW YOUR TIPPING POINTS

"The tipping point is the magic moment when an idea, trend or social behaviour crosses a threshold, tips and spreads like wildfire."
Malcolm Gladwell

You are standing in a queue waiting for tickets to an entertainment show that you have wanted to attend *forever*. You have also promised your life partner that you will meet them at a definite time and place to celebrate something special.

The queue is taking ages to move. Time is slipping away quickly and you are going to need to leave soon to make this treasured meeting.

Your mind is racing, trying to decide at what point you leave so that you don't disappoint the most significant person in your life.

You may contact your life partner and find out how late you can be for your meeting. You may try to assess how long the queue is going to take. You know there is a definite time that you may have to leave, and forego your tickets.

This is a simple example of a tipping point, and we have all experienced similar dilemmas.

The tipping point is the critical juncture in an evolving situation that is a turning point in the development of that process.

Life is full of tipping points, and as a leader it is important to identify these points because they are often the times that you are required to be the most decisive.

In this chapter, I discuss some of the aspects of tipping points that I believe are relevant to you as a woman leader, and provide some guidance in dealing with these.

Aspects addressed include:

- Life is not a contest.
- Setting boundaries.
- Outsource what you can.
- Knowing when you are at your limit.
- How to say NO nicely to protect your YES.
- Finding good mentors, champions and venting partners.

Life is not a contest

"If you compare yourself with others, you may become vain and bitter; for always there will be greater and lesser persons than yourself."
Desiderata

When my daughter was born, I had just become the owner of my accounting practice because my business partner had died. The birth of my daughter was one of those truly amazing and exhilarating moments in life, as well as one of the most challenging.

As most new mothers will tell you, there is no training or advice that can prepare you for the complete change that happens to you physically, mentally and emotionally. It is just something that needs to be experienced. I do, however, wish I knew all that I know now about the physical and emotional changes that happen to a woman's body through the birthing process. I discussed this in Chapter 3, 'Know Your Playing Field'.

I believe if I had have known this, I might have been kinder to myself. Instead, I proceeded to think that I had to be the best mother, best wife and, of course, best business person. I don't know who I needed to prove this to though. This resulted in me being full of anxiety about my daughter and full of anxiety about my business, which I couldn't turn off.

I know some of the angst was created by who I am and my need to have everything right in life. There also were my clients' expectations and I was the main income earner.

Other misgivings came about because of my own beliefs about what society expected from me as a mother, based on the many messages that I received from family, friends and society in general, and lots of messages that I perceived through this time.

My former husband also thought that giving birth to a child meant you were automatically programmed to know what to do as a mother.

When my daughter was about two and a half, I nearly came totally unstuck through a period of depression. Fortunately, I knew I needed help and I had a medical doctor who assisted me, as well as a good friend who directed me to a wonderful psychologist. As these professionals pointed out, the depression wasn't entirely caused by the birth of my daughter. In the two years prior to her arrival, both my father and my close business partner had died. Life events had converged with some tough emotional issues that I had to work through.

I recovered quickly and vowed I would never go back to that black hole ever again.

There were many lessons learned through this very difficult period in life and the main one was that life is not a contest. It is a journey, and more than that, it is *your* journey.

I've told this story to illustrate that false tipping points can be created because of the perceived messages you are receiving about how life should be lived for you and your family.

This is especially true when it comes to your parenting skills, especially being a mother. Because we are still the predominant caregivers, the success of our children can be intrinsically linked to the success of us as mothers.

Parenting is the most challenging job that we undertake without proper training – and definitely with minimal moral support. It's easy to go down the track of thinking that if your children behave badly then you are a bad mother – and therefore your children and you are just plain bad.

Often the messages come from the people that are closest – maybe from your mother or mother-in-law, for example, because of their expectations of parenting.

These are some of my tips to chase away these crazy expectations:

- Are your children healthy, safe, happy and engaging in the world in a positive way? If yes, then it doesn't matter what type of the parenting methods you are using because these methods are working at the level that matters. Our parents and parents-in-laws grew up in a different era, so their context of how the world operates is totally different to what is happening in your world. As an example, they may have stayed at home to look after the children and the home, whereas you are trying to look after the children and the home and your career.

- Don't engage in competition about the development of your children because it's a competition you cannot win. Every child is different and develops in their own time. It's better to spend your energy really knowing and understanding your children's individual characteristics so you can help them grow into healthy, happy and engaged adults.

- All decisions are family decisions. This means that the children's livelihood needs to be balanced with the safety, health and care of everyone in the family. By having this as a guide for your family, you will ensure that your children learn that their higher needs may have to be compromised to fit with everyone in the family, and especially you. This will be a valuable life skill for your children to learn, as they will be part of teams for the rest of their life.

Setting boundaries

One of the basics for building trust between you, your family and any teams with which you are working, is having clear boundaries around your responsibilities and those of others in the group or family.

A boundary is something that separates two things: walls and fences are clearly material boundaries, so how do you create non-material separation?

One way to do this in your close relationships is to visualise a line between two people.

A healthy relationship occurs when both parties take responsibility for forming the line and do what they are both responsible for in that relationship. If one person steps over the line to do what the other person should do, it results in unclear roles and may undermine a person's autonomy. If one person remains distant from the line and defaults on what is their responsibility, it results in withdrawal or disengagement for everyone.

The challenging part in assessing boundaries is deciding what belongs to you and what belongs to another person in the family. How you sort that out will determine how you choose to communicate and what you attend to.

With open communication about how you want boundaries in your family to be set, along with lots of practice, you can build much healthier relationships that are respectful, safe and meaningful.

Boundaries in close relationships are often more blurred than in working situations. In organisations, every person has a position description that sets out the clear boundaries around their role.

Many of the same principles apply though – effective communication, trust, and respect, which are discussed in Chapter 6, 'Basic Skills Required'.

What you may find though is that with everyday routine,

you may want to step over the line rather than have the tough conversation about who is responsible for the job that you are doing. It may seem easier to have peace by doing it yourself rather than create conflict by addressing responsibilities.

I was a single mother for all of my daughter's teenage years. When I got home at night, after a long day at the business, I often walked away from difficult conversations with her for peace, quiet and ease of spirit. Invariably, though, I paid the price for not having the tough conversation because the boundary line of responsibility became more and more blurred and then it became even tougher to strengthen my position concerning what was required of my daughter.

You may also be tempted to walk over the line because you believe you know more about parenting than your life partner.

When my daughter was born, my former husband became the predominant carer for her because I was the main income earner. I remember often coming home from the office to find my tiny infant daughter asleep on the change mat on the dining room table while my husband was in the kitchen cooking. My first instinct was to question why she was not in her cot in her room asleep. This seemed more logical to me for my daughter's comfort.

I deliberately stopped myself from reacting because the agreed boundary line was that he was responsible for the care of our daughter and so long as my daughter was safe and well cared for, the methodology was not for me to comment on.

Again, I applied the principle I explained earlier. I asked the question – is my daughter healthy, happy and safe? If the answer was yes, then I would deliberately put the matter out of my mind.

There are always plenty of other things to do and worry about when you have children.

I have seen other mothers interfere in how husbands go about caring for their children when the women have expressly asked for help. As a result of this interference the men typically became confused about what was required of them, and their autonomy became undermined. Then the mothers complained that their husbands wouldn't be involved in the caring to give them a break.

The boundary line had become blurred and the husbands had disengaged. It is extremely difficult to strengthen things again when disengagement has happened.

Another question you could ask yourself – do I want this task or responsibility back on my side of the line? If no, then be quiet and observe only. We all have different ways of going about something. So long as the outcome is satisfactory, it doesn't matter the route. It is not a contest to see who has the best method.

This concept of boundaries applies for any relationship, including teams at work or volunteering – any project that requires an outcome. As a leader, it will be necessary to determine the responsibilities for each person on the team and ensure that each person steps up to the line of responsibility. You will also need to observe if someone is stepping over the line into someone else's responsibilities.

Once you have these clear boundaries, it is much easier to have kind and constructive conversations about what has not been done or, more importantly, celebrate what has been done well.

Outsource what you can

Not long after my daughter was little, I had an "ah ha" moment after a weekend of cleaning and tidying our home. I thought to myself, "I have just worked a 60-hour week with my business and have cared for our daughter, plus tried to find time with my husband *and then* spent the whole weekend cleaning and tidying our home. This is crazy." The next week I employed a cleaner.

Similarly, my former husband was spending all his time child caring and trying to spend some time working towards his business – so we employed a gardener to mow the lawns and look after our gardens.

Outsourcing these two jobs meant we had more time for each other and ourselves, as well as our delightful, developing and fun daughter.

Remember, I said it does not matter how the outcome occurs, what matters is that it happens. No one is going to give you an award for exhaustion.

Of course, you might be thinking that you cannot afford this expense. I have seen families grapple with this. The question is usually around childcare, so the woman can go back to work.

Often, I see the short-term reality of being cash neutral during the childcare years given as the reason why woman don't go back to work. (Of course, there may be many valid reasons for not going back to work.) My point is, don't take the short-term view and just focus on a few years of being cash neutral. If you do return to work, after that period, when your child is at school, you will have held onto your career and the cash position will improve. Hopefully your career will have expanded as well and there will be increased salary to compensate for the early cash shortage.

It is much more challenging to re-enter a career after a break away. I was out of the accounting profession for 15 months when I was the Financial Controller of the private hospital. When I returned to work, the learning curve to get up to speed with the income tax changes in that short period was enormous. Change happens much faster now as well.

You may be thinking that it is your responsibility as a woman to look after your home and keep it clean and welcoming. You may have people close to you who shame you into thinking that you are a lesser person because you are not doing it yourself. Remember, don't listen to these people. You are the one living your life. Your family, your life partner and you are far more important than you personally cleaning your home.

Knowing when you are at your limit

Life is complex and complicated. This is not to say that it hasn't always been this way through human history. The difference now is that we receive so many messages about who we are supposed to be, with graphic visual cues as well.

Vision is our number one sense, so to have this sense constantly bombarded with visual messages is stressful. These messages tell you how you are supposed to look, how you are supposed to act and what constitutes success.

Then you need to walk through your own self-control minefield to achieve goals, stay mentally and physically healthy, and have a purposeful life. We know that working on all of this does mean a more satisfying life. It also means that at various points it can be totally overwhelming.

In Chapter 3, 'Know your Playing Field', I discuss the importance of a good hormone balance between testosterone and cortisol. If you feel that your cortisol level has risen to the maximum limit for you, my recommendation is that, if possible, you try to step back from everything and have a break. Time out can be a wonderful de-stressor.

I often felt that my stress levels were like a pressure cooker. When I felt that the pressure valve was really, really tight and ready to blow, I knew that I needed to step back and take some time to relax.

Of course, it may not be entirely possible to have a complete break. I know when my daughter was little and I was running the business, the most I could allow myself was a one-hour massage each week and a 20-minute walk most mornings. I made certain that these were scheduled into my week and day though, so that the activity actually happened.

I've covered some other techniques in more depth in Chapter 12, 'Nourishment and Replenishment', but I will mention a few here that neuroscience has proven.

Emotions can be regulated more effectively by finding the right words to describe what you are feeling. I have found that having a journal helps. I write in this book when frustration is high, not necessarily every day. I even have called it my 'pity' journal because I only seem to write in it when I'm frustrated and need to de-stress, or I need to understand my thoughts on a topic.

Mindfulness is also being shown as a wonderful technique for having non-judgemental awareness of what one is thinking, feeling and experiencing. This again is a labelling technique, which seems to act as a mental braking-system for stress.

Further in this section, I discuss having a team around you for support. I suggest mentors, champions and venting partners.

I find that a venting partner is a good friend to have. This is a person who can listen to your emotional unload in a non-judgemental way. Sometimes just voicing the words around emotions and situations allows you to see a course of action for change or even a way of just letting off steam.

As a leader, it is so important to know when you are at your limit, because when you are stressed you lose perspective on what needs to be done and you are prone to making inappropriate statements.

Saying No to protect your Yes

You will see in the section on 'Building Trust' in Chapter 6, 'Basic Skills Required', that two of the key elements of trustworthiness are reliability and accountability. You cannot be reliable and accountable if you continually say yes to everything and fill your life to a point where you cannot function.

It is much easier to say yes than no, especially if you like someone and you feel that you want to help them. Our role, as women, has been to be carers and supporters, and with those roles comes this tendency to think that we are available for everyone, often at our own physical and mental wellbeing.

However, saying No to protect your Yes means that you will always be able to deliver what you say you are going to deliver. This is the cornerstone of reliability and accountability.

You need to carefully consider what you are trying to achieve with your life, who is important in your life, and your own capability and capacity. Your earlier work around 'Knowing Yourself' and 'Knowing Your Why' will give you a clear indication of what you want to bring into your life for the fulfilment of your life's purpose.

Most people are comfortable when another person says no. You are admired for being clear about what you can and cannot achieve. This is certainly much better than promising more than you can deliver.

One way you can assist someone when you know you are going to deny their request is to consider whether you know someone who may be able to assist them instead. This can soften the impact.

Also, you might know that you cannot do what is being asked of you right now; however, you may be able to do it in the future. You could ask if there is a deadline for the work that needs to be done. Just be careful that you don't clutter your future with too much as well.

You can also be supportive by checking later to see if the person has found someone to assist. This is another way of softening your no.

I think all of us have experienced a situation where someone has overpromised and not delivered, and know how frustrating that can be for a project or general work and family situations.

Finding good mentors, champions and venting partners

One of the really strange paradoxes about being human is that most people like to help other people, but most people don't like to ask for help.

Certainly, asking for help does make you feel vulnerable and somehow lesser as a person. Yet as you will see in Chapter 7, 'Practice, Practice, Practice', obtaining good feedback is critical to learning and improved performance.

I wish I had allowed myself to be more vulnerable earlier in my career and built a support network of good mentors, champions and venting partners. I'm sure I would have reached my goals easier and sooner.

In the introduction to this book I wrote about sitting at the table for 25 years with nine men and realising that I was not included in the power dynamic of the group. I realise now I should have asked one of them to be my champion, which would have given me a way into the power dynamic. It would have cracked open the unconscious bias a little more.

Who is a good champion?

My first business partner was a good champion. I would hear him praising my accounting skills and business abilities to our clients. He never hesitated to include me in client meetings, where he would confer with me about what needed to be done for that client from a business perspective, so that the client could see my abilities firsthand. He did not seem to see my gender at all. He just saw a very capable accountant who could help his clients.

These clients ultimately became my clients when he died

sooner than we expected. Because the clients knew my previous partner's respect for me as an accountant, most of them remained my clients after his death and I have worked with most of them for 30 years.

Given the statistics reflecting gender equality currently in Australia, you may well find yourself in a situation where you may be in a gender minority at the senior level.

If that case arises, I would recommend that you find a man that you respect and that obviously respects you, and ask them to champion you during important decisions. This is certainly important where you do not think your ideas are going to be heard because of bias.

I have sat at many board tables and expressed very valid ideas, and often seen that, until they are reiterated by a man, those ideas are not heard. This is extremely frustrating but so true. Sorry guys!

If you find yourself in a similar situation, approach the person you would like to champion you outside the board table dynamic and share your ideas. If they are supportive, you ask them to show that support at the board table and acknowledge your contribution. You will find that this is a more positive outcome for you. A point to note is that it needs to be someone who will acknowledge your contribution and not someone on their own ego trip who takes the credit.

If there are other women at the table, support each other's ideas where possible. Make a point of mentioning that these women have made an important point and should be heard.

I often gave up expressing ideas when I wasn't being heard, and I walked away from the table totally frustrated with the process. I even walked away from groups because of my frustration.

You may feel you need to find a champion in many situations where unconscious bias exists.

Who is a good mentor?

The definition of a mentor is an experienced and trusted advisor. It is usually someone who is older and wiser, and who can impart life, business and/or personal and business skills to you so that you can move through the various life minefields without being destroyed or maimed.

I have used the word mentor rather than coach because a coach is likely to instruct you on what to do or say in a particular situation. A mentor is someone who guides rather than instructs.

A mentor will still provide a framework for improvement. It should, however, be suitable for your actual issues and your processes rather than fit with the mentor's belief of how to do something.

My first business partner was also a good mentor. He would listen attentively and empathetically and make constructive suggestions of methods or ways I could try. I would then express what I thought would work best for me to bring about change.

It's not easy being a mentor for men. Their historic roles have been the providers and protectors. Their automatic default is to fix something or find a solution for a problem. They also don't want to deal with heavy emotion because they have been encouraged from an early age to suppress or veneer over what they are feeling. They are also logical and know that emotion can get in the way of clear decisions.

It's not easy being a mentor for women either because sometimes we tend to want to wallow in emotion rather than guide the mentee out of the situation.

You want someone as a mentor who can be empathetic about your problem while not stepping over the line into solution mode. They need to allow you to work through whatever is happening so hopefully you will arrive at a solution yourself. Once you can see the way forward, you are more likely to make the necessary changes in your life that will bring a viable solution. This allows you autonomy and a boundary on your responsibility.

Empathy is one of those words, like compassion, which can imply vulnerability. Your emotions may be triggered by what the other person is sharing with you. Most of us don't like feeling that we are out of control emotionally – and we can feel that we are unable to manage what is happening to us. It's much easier to walk away or just be sympathetic.

Brené Brown has a wonderful video about the difference between empathy and sympathy that highlights what happens with each of these approaches to an issue.

This is available on YouTube as *Brené Brown on Empathy.*[18]

She highlights four elements of empathy, which I have summarised below.

- Perspective taking – the ability to be able to see the issue from the other person's point of view and recognise the person's truth about what is happening for them.

- Staying out of judgement about the person's emotion or situation.
- Recognising the emotion in the other person.
- Then communicating that.

This means that you connect with the emotion within you that reflects what the other person is feeling, so you can appropriately express that you understand what is happening for them.

This is very scary for most of us because we have probably not addressed the emotion for ourselves, yet alone for someone else. We would rather turn away from the situation than step in and connect.

Sympathy is where you try to silver-line something, and usually people express it by beginning with the phrase, "At least …". You've had a miscarriage – a sympathetic response – "At least, you know that you can get pregnant." Empathetic response – "I cannot imagine the feeling of loss that you are experiencing at this time. You are brave to share and I'm honoured that you wanted to share this with me."

Empathy creates connection and this is what you need from the person you choose as your mentor. You need them to know you well enough that they can guide you to improve, change or deal with a difficult leadership situation – whatever is going on for you.

Your mentor should require accountability from you as well, which is where the framework comes into play. You need to try very hard to implement what you have determined through the mentoring process or you have just wasted time for both of you.

Become a mentor for other young women leaders. Mentoring

is a wonderful way to learn how to guide and inspire – it's the cornerstone of leadership.

Who is a good venting partner?

I think a good venting partner is someone who will let you emotionally download, will not judge what you are saying and will wallow with you for a bit in the emotion, but not too much.

We are emotional creatures. I also believe that as women we are required to be much more in tune with our emotions than men because of the caring nature of the roles that we have traditionally undertaken. Caring requires empathy and as I said earlier, empathy requires you to recognise emotions in another person and communicate them. You also need to be able to recognise it in yourself so that you don't get drawn into the other person's emotional vortex.

Emotions are your responses to the continuously updated situations that are happening to you in your current environment.

From a neuroscience stance, we have a two-brain system that is constantly appraising whether things are a threat, and mobilising various aspects of our body as an emotional response to that appraisal. Do you need to run, freeze or fight?

Your amygdala is the little cluster of nuclei buried in the depths of your temporal lobe. It is an old structure in evolutionary terms and its special emphasis is on detecting threats.

Then you have the insula, which is a cortical region folded underneath the frontal and temporal lobes. The insula has a map of what it is going on with your internal organs and will determine what needs to happen in your body when responding to emotion and painful sensations. The insula is especially involved with negative emotions that have a strong bodily component, such as disgust.

Emotions do not just start and stop. They are cyclical, depending on the continued inputs and your response to what is happening to you. Your emotional responses would be enormously different if you stepped into a difficult situation, as opposed to walking away from the same situation. If you step in, you are likely to experience anger, frustration and confusion. If you walk away, you are likely to experience disappointment, frustration and inferiority.

By having a venting partner, you can look at your emotional reactions to particular situations and perhaps consider different response processes for similar events in the future. As we discussed earlier, finding your words can be a good way to brake the brain and reduce stress. Finding the appropriate words to describe emotions is so important for the regulation of emotions. Discussions with your venting partner may allow the best words to emerge.

Of course, any of these discussions must be totally focused on a positive outcome, and not just create an emotional pity-party just for the sake of it. You need to manage your emotions and not allow them to escalate into any kind of victim mentality.

Your venting partner needs to be emotionally intelligent and able to help you explore things in your discussions – and vice versa. They also need to be willing to keep your conversations in a vault, i.e. not share with anyone inappropriately. This venting partner must understand the importance of your stories and that you are the only person qualified to share them. I discuss the 'vault' concept further in Chapter 6, 'Basic Skill Required' in the section, 'Building Trust'.

Your personal team of supporters

As a leader, I would thoroughly recommend that you spend some time building these relationships in your life to help you through the challenges of just being human, really. It will translate into better leadership decisions as well as personal growth. Your team of supporters will also hopefully help you deal with the tipping points in your leadership role and life.

Summary

- The tipping point is the critical moment in an evolving situation that leads to new and irreversible change. Life is full of tipping points and as a leader it is important to be able to identify these points because they are often the times that you are required to be the most decisive.
- I have looked at some aspects of tipping points that I believe are relevant for you as a woman leader: life is not a contest; setting boundaries; knowing when you are at your limit; learning how to say No nicely to protect your Yes; finding good mentors, champions and venting partners.
- Observe the tipping points in your life and discover your own methods for getting through these critical junctures. Make certain you work on building your support crew who can help you to survive and thrive through these points in your life and leadership journey.

CHAPTER FIVE

BASIC STEPS

> "Dream, Believe, Do, Repeat."
> Audrey Assad

Once you have decided on your leadership project you will need to consider how you are going to go about it. Most projects we undertake in life take a similar process, which I have set out in the diagram below:

Basic Steps Process

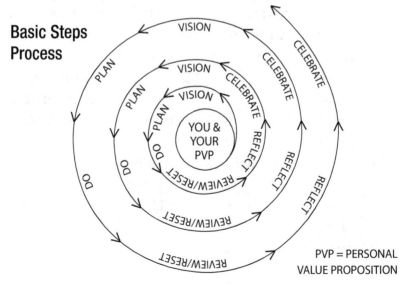

PVP = PERSONAL VALUE PROPOSITION

I believe these steps can be applied to almost anything you want to achieve in your life, including one-off projects, or new learning and continuous assignments, such as writing a book or running a business.

This chapter looks closely at the systematic process I have designed for achieving the outcomes that you want for your leadership project and your life. It takes you step-by-step through the different stages, to success.

Vision

Good leaders know that it is important to have a clear vision of what they would like to happen, as well as where they are now. This is a critical starting point for you. The clearer you can envision what you want to achieve, the more likely it is to happen.

In Chapter 7, 'Practice, Practice, Practice', I take you through the neuroscience of what occurs in your mind when you have a clear vision. Your mind automatically starts to look for what is needed to make your goal happen. Your mind wants you to be happy so it will work subconsciously to make that occur. You suddenly see resources everywhere and people appear that you may not have noticed before.

It is also best that you document this vision in precise language, including the emotions you are going to experience as you finally make what you want to happen eventuate. It is well known that if we document a plan we are more than likely going to complete it. It can be in dot points and concise. It just needs to be documented.

Make certain that you have a compelling 'why' for the project. As explained in my earlier chapter, 'Know Your Why', when you have a reason for doing something that you passionately believe in, you have a clear path to follow. When you have a clear path to follow, you can always come back to it when you get side-tracked. And you will be side-tracked, believe me. That is the reality of our current world and who we are as humans. When you find that you have spun off into another realm, you can seek out the path you have set and bring yourself back to your course.

Another way to make a project compelling might be to look at the emotional cost to you if it is not completed. You may also want to look at the barriers that can potentially stop you achieving what you set out to do, and consider them when you come to set realistic goals in the planning phase. There may be new skills you need to learn to be able to achieve your vision.

Create lots of "If ... Then ..." statements to help prevent detours from the path and quell any self-doubt that may arise.

Some examples might be:

- If I become side-tracked, I will think about my vision and feel the joy of how my achievement will feel.
- If I doubt my abilities, I will remember what I have already done and apply the same principles to what I am doing now.
- If I don't have what I need, I will look for the resources required.
- If I need support, I will ask for help from my supportive network.

If you are leading a team or a business, the vision you create will need to be embedded in the overall culture and values for the team or business. It is important to involve as many people as you can to determine this vision so that it is an acceptable one that can easily be adopted by all. If you can get them to express their own words and emotions around this vision, it is more likely to remain a clear path for them as well.

Sometimes when you take on a leadership role the vision and culture might already be in place and you just need to make certain that it fits you. Hopefully, you will have already considered this as part of weighing up your acceptance of the role.

You will no doubt have to create visions and plans for other projects within these types of organisations and businesses, so use this vision idea for these projects.

Remember also that your project needs to suit who you are and your Personal Value Proposition (PVP). If these two elements are not being satisfied by a project, you will soon lose interest.

When I decided to write this book, I knew that I wanted to help young women see the benefits in being a leader because of the thrill of contribution that I had experienced in my leadership journey. This was my 'why' for the book.

I had no idea how to go about writing a book, and then a journalist joined my Laughter Yoga exercise group – so I asked her what I should do. She directed me to Bev Ryan, my book mentor and publishing project manager.

Bev advised me to survey both men and women to find out their thoughts and concerns about leadership. I also interviewed several men and women for their specific viewpoints and ideas.

This body of work then assisted me to develop a book structure, and suddenly I had a clear path to follow to achieve my vision.

I also wrote down a vision of me holding my book in my hand and envisioned the emotions I would feel seeing it there.

I used all of this to keep me writing and, believe me, writing a book is a long, challenging and arduous project.

When the words wouldn't flow or the self-doubt about the worth of this project entered my head, I thought about my vision of holding my book in my hand. I re-visited my plan and my 'why' for the book. Then, I felt compelled to sit and do something for the project, even if it was only some reading: I then waited and hoped for the words to come, which they usually did.

As I said in Chapter 2, 'Know Your Why', this book fits perfectly into my Life Sentence – PVP. I have also used my most important Character Strengths of curiosity and love of learning while researching and writing this book. Although it has been arduous and challenging, I have enjoyed the process because it fits with who I am. It definitely feels good.

Plan

In this step you break your vision down into smaller realistic goals and set deadlines and measurements to ensure you keep the project going. (In the next chapter, 'Basic Skills Required', I set out a process for setting realistic goals.)

At the planning stage, you will need to look at what resources you are going to require, what new skills you may need to learn, and who you will need to involve. You will need to consider any barriers that may arise and stop achievement.

Establish clear guidelines for the people who are going to be involved. You will need to portray self-confidence, build trust for the team and have effective communication and delegation skills. These concepts are also discussed in the next chapter.

Established systems and processes make any project easier. Learning happens with repeated routines that layer the learning, putting new skills on top of earlier learned ones. You will need to have plans for developing the systems you require.

The structure I developed for this book allowed me to determine the chapters I was going to write. I then noted ideas for each chapter – I had broken the overall vision into smaller chunks that were more manageable for me to write.

I set an overall deadline for having my book in my hand. This, however, did get changed, which I will discuss later. Still, having that first deadline did make me focus and begin.

Do

"Everything is hard before it is easy."
Goethe

In the words of the Nike advertisement – Just Do It! This is where the rubber hits the road and you act on the goals that you have set in the planning stage.

Hopefully, if there are precise systems and processes to follow, the doing will be easy.

When you are learning a new skill, or starting a new project, your fear of failure can be great. Once you start and you see some progress (any progress really), your self-confidence grows. It is then just a case of keeping the momentum going.

Once I wrote my first section for the book, I felt a sense of liberation and confidence that I could do this. I was going to write this book! I established some times for routine writing and I endeavoured to stick to this routine.

Review and reset

The 'doing' step always results in changes to the plans, systems and processes diligently created earlier. It may mean that you need to review your deadlines. It may be that the action you take brings the wrong results. It may mean you want to abandon the original vision. It may mean you need to make changes to the systems and processes.

When working on big projects or running a business, you will need to make certain that the people overseeing teams have the skills to assess the effectiveness of the action being taken. You will also need to make certain they can build their team members' abilities to self-review their own work. In the next chapter I discuss the important aspects of building collaborative, diverse and inclusive teams.

Feedback is an important part of deliberate practice, leading to learning and improvement. It is essential for peak performance. Top athletes and musicians seek it constantly to ensure their best outcomes. Everyone, including you, needs to be encouraged to become comfortable with seeking and receiving feedback.

The first casualty of my book plan was my deadline. I had wanted to write the book in one year. Life intervened, as it does, and I had some work and personal matters, which took priority at various times during that year. These matters meant I didn't have as much time to write as I would have liked, and my creativity diminished while I was dealing with the emotions resulting from these life events.

Also, most of us are not very good at determining the actual amount of time required to achieve a project. I tend to always be over-ambitious when thinking about what I can achieve in the time that I have.

The next change of plan for my book project came about when I reviewed the times that I had allocated for my writing time. I found that, with my weekly workload, I did not have the mental capacity to do any effective or creative writing during the week. I had to devote one day of my weekend to writing.

I then found that the regular routine of writing made me stale and de-motivated. So I began using my writing as an opportunity to visit different places. I went to my favourite art gallery where I reviewed the artwork and then sat and wrote for a few hours. I went to my favourite beach for a walk and then wrote.

I like travel and finding new places, so adding a journey to my writing session was a fabulous way of combining what I had to do with what I like doing.

I have reviewed my vision for this book many, many times during its creation. Thankfully, I never lost my excitement and belief associated with why I wanted to write the book. This was always a wonderful incentive to keep going.

I remember another time when I had a vision of walking the Inca trail in Peru to Machu Picchu. I knew that I had to be physically fit and strong to make this vision happen. My plan to reach this goal was to join a bush club and do some trekking with them over a long period to get fit.

Our orientation instructor took us on what he described as an easy bushwalk. I was absolutely exhausted. I was the slowest person on the trails. Also, I discovered that I now actually disliked intense bush trekking, even though I loved it when I was younger. This experience resulted in me revising my first vision.

I still haven't given up on going back to visit Machu Picchu. It just means that I may not walk the Inca trail. I believe in never saying never though.

That exercise made me realise that I needed to first lose some weight to be physically fitter. I also needed to find a walking group that wasn't as fixated on the trekking and the physical challenge as the first group I joined. I have had to reset that particular project vision and plan.

Throughout the writing of this book, I have provided some of my work to various people in my support network for comment. Armed with their positive feedback, I kept writing. Positive review and feedback is always essential.

Reflect

Insight happens in moments of quiet, neuroscientists have established. Our brains collect a huge amount of data and ideas, and when we have quiet moments, the mind puts all of this disparate data and these ideas together to create our ah-ha moments!

In fact, our greatest insights can happen when we are doing something totally unrelated, such as taking a shower.

My first experience of this amazing phenomena came when I was a school student, and doing my math homework. I struggled and struggled to find the answer to a particular math equation. Giving up in frustration, I went to play the piano. As I was playing, the answer to this equation hit my mind. The ah-ha moment was so great that I jumped up from the piano stool and raced out to my homework. I'm sure I must have even shouted something like "Eureka", or its equivalent. My mother thought something terrible had happened to me and came running to see what was wrong.

Planning, doing and reviewing take lots of brainpower. It's sometimes challenging to see the wood from the trees. It can be almost impossible to be creative. I would recommend that you schedule time in your week just for reflecting. If you can do something totally different from your regular routine, then even better. Go for a walk in the park, play with your children or even meditate. In Chapter 11, 'Nourishment and Replenishment', I review the scientific benefits of mindful meditation.

Organisations such as Google and Facebook have embraced this important creative brain requirement and encourage time-out in their office environments. They have lots of breakout areas for their staff to just play and reflect.

Your reflection time can be used to note all the new learnings you have had from the planning, doing and reviewing stages: these new learnings can then be fed back into the process again.

This is why I have designed the process image to expand outwards from the centre, as a spiral that grows.

New learning needs to be layered onto previous workable learning. This is how the mind expands and grows.

Celebrate

As humans, we are nurtured by a certain amount of ritual, celebration and ceremony. Celebration of milestones on a project can contribute to renewed enthusiasm for finding answers or for completion – or even just reinforcing the organisation's culture.

Psychologist William David said, "The deepest craving in human beings is the need to be appreciated". Everyone wants respect and recognition.

As a leader, you need to be aware of this basic human need and make certain that you give praise and positive recognition to your team members. It can be as simple as a smile and an informal chat about their life. Encourage your team members to contribute their ideas and praise them for wanting to make your project or organisation better.

Remember to appreciate the people who have significantly contributed to your success as well.

There will be much celebration for me when this book is printed and in my hands. And it most certainly would not have happened without the support that I have had along the way. It is a pleasure to acknowledge my wonderful support people in this book in my Acknowledgements page. The final way to thank them will be to celebrate with these same people at the book's launch.

Leadership courses

I believe leadership needs to be learned. There are always the few who appear to have innate leadership skills but, for most of us, it is learning and practice that makes us successful. I have reinforced this point in Chapter 7, 'Practice, Practice, Practice'.

One course that I would recommend that is relatively inexpensive is the Toastmasters International High Performance Leadership Program.[19] It sets out the six major dimensions of Service Leadership, which are:

- Vision and Values
- Direction
- Persuasion
- Support
- Development
- Appreciation

If this appeals to you, join a Toastmasters club and undertake this program, as it will provide a systematic approach to leadership that has practical steps to follow. It will provide a good starting point for your life-long leadership journey.

I will also soon have leadership courses and resources available at my website – www.denise-gibbons.com.[20]

Summary

Remember to anchor your project to who you are by considering your Life Sentence – PVP, and make certain that it fits with your 'why'. This will ensure that you enjoy the journey even if the outcome is not entirely what you expected.

- Take the time to reflect on the learning that you have made during the project, because our minds develop and expand by layering new learning on top of previous workable learning.
- Celebration is important to keep enthusiasm going for projects, so ensure that you build these occasions into your project.
- My recommendation is to have a systematic process for every leadership (and life) project of vision – plan, do, review and reset, reflect and celebrate. Having these defined steps means that you are more likely to achieve the outcome that you want.
- Leadership needs to be learnt so find courses that suit you to keep this learning going.

CHAPTER SIX

BASIC LEADERSHIP SKILLS REQUIRED

> "Do unto others as you would have them do unto you."
> Luke 6:31

If leadership in its purest form is to guide and inspire others, then the skills required are fundamentally about understanding yourself and people. This is the cornerstone of my definition of Service Leadership.

In this chapter, I explore some of the basic skills that I believe are essential to becoming a successful woman leader. Many of these fit into the Toastmaster's leadership definition. The need for other skills will emerge from knowing yourself, knowing your 'why', as well as completing the project you are leading and the learning you make along your journey.

With any skill, it is necessary to incorporate them into your life. As I've advocated throughout the book, practicing these skills is important. At the end of each section, I have noted suggestions for putting them into practice in your life.

Each moment of layered learning makes us who we are, as you will discover in the next chapter 'Practice, Practice, Practice'.

Self-confidence

My Pilates teacher explained that by slightly destabilising the body and holding it strong through the sensation of loss of control, or in other words, the wobbly bit (as I call it), you strengthen the muscles and the body.

Anyone who has experienced Pilates or Yoga will relate to what I'm talking about. If you haven't experienced these forms of exercise, you probably have used stretching as a warm up or warm down for general exercise. If so, you will know that moment where you feel that you are not quite able to hold everything steady. It may only be a few seconds, if you are an experienced athlete, but it happens for all of us.

Continuing to hold through that time of uncertainty leads to a sense of power and strength in Pilates and Yoga, and a sense of release when stretching.

Giving up when you are in the middle of the wobbly bit results in a feeling that nothing is happening. It's almost like you have wasted your time and effort. You wonder why you have bothered. I believe this is a fabulous analogy for building mental and emotional confidence.

It requires mental and emotional fortitude to hold through the moments of uncertainty, self-doubt and fear (the wobbly bits) until you pass through to the point of achievement, accomplishment and triumph.

Self-confidence and wisdom come from deep learning, which comes from holding strong through the destabilising moments, until we have triumphed.

The ingredients that are important for developing

self-confidence are:

- Having the knowledge that you, as a person, are important and that a wholehearted life is your purpose. (*I am good enough and what I do matters!*)
- Making realistic goals for the various important parts of your life. (*I know what to do and I can do this!*)
- Capturing the moments when you hold through the uncertainty, fear and self-doubt to achievement of these goals. (*Wow! I did it!*)
- Noting the learning from the hold moments for future reference. (*What did I learn with this process?*)
- Celebrating and reflecting on the process so that the learning becomes a part of who you are. (*I share the experience and remember the jolts of joy!*)

Each day as you work on your self-confidence, you discover hope. Hope is not an emotion; it is a cognitive way of thinking that is born out of the process of self-confidence.

When you believe that you can do something you feel hopeful, which gives you a sense of optimism, joy and unlimited possibilities. Filled with this belief in yourself, you can focus on what needs to be done to move towards your goals. Once you have started achieving some of the parts of your goals, you become more confident and so the process takes a circulatory momentum. You start to trust your abilities to be able to achieve. I discuss the skill of building trust later in this chapter.

My experience has been that self-confidence waxes and wanes depending on what is happening in your life. For example, when you are unwell, life narrows right down to a moment-by-moment existence. Self-confidence is the first casualty of physical illness. Your perseverance is spent working towards being well again so that you can recapture the beauty of life again and your life's purpose.

Life is a continuum so you may have to revisit this skill many times.

These are your practice steps:

Look at what you have achieved

1. Sit down and make a list of what you have achieved to date in your life.
2. Note down any obstacles that you had to overcome.
3. Find words for the emotions that arose through the process, both good and bad.
4. Note the Character Strengths used for your achievement. How did you stay strong?

Look at what you want to achieve

1. Make a list of what you want to achieve in your life.
2. Note the Character Strengths from the exercise above that may help you achieve these goals.
3. Look at the next section on realistic goal setting.
4. Set up "If ... Then ..." scenarios to keep you on track.
5. Look at the elements of trust to help you stay strong.
6. Ask a mentor or friend to either be part of the goal or keep you accountable.

Realistic goal setting

Goal setting is important for any project you want to achieve in life. It is also an essential ingredient in building self-confidence.

Goal setting is easy. Setting realistic goals that you will achieve is not so easy.

As an example, you might decide that you want to be a triathlete. You see this as the way to become physically fit. Certainly this is an admirable goal and well worth working towards.

However, if you have just given birth to your first child, you work full-time and you have a wonderful life partner, you need to question whether becoming a triathlete at this point in your life is a realistic goal. A more realistic goal might be that you will walk half-an-hour each day with your baby or even enjoy 15 minutes of meditation and stretching.

There needs to be goal congruence with the rest of your life or you will not succeed at the goal you have set.

If you set your goal as a triathlete and you find that you cannot achieve this because of what happens everyday in your life, you are more than likely going to give up on physical exercise altogether. Your reaction might be – "Oh! This is all too hard! It's not worth doing anything!"

The negative self-talk will inevitably kick in at this point. You will tell yourself that you can't do this, you will *never* (that magic absolute word that solidifies everything) be able to do this and, as a result, you won't be bothered with physical exercise at all because it is all too difficult.

You do not want to damage your self-confidence by having unrealistic goals. You do not want to feel that you are untrustworthy.

The basic ingredients of realistic goal setting are as follows:

1. Determine your goals.
There are two important parts to defining a goal:

- Make your goal specific. Goals should be measurable and have an end point.
- Make your goals realistic. Taking on challenges can be really motivating, but don't set yourself up to fail. If you're not sure if your goal is realistic, talk to someone you trust about it.

2. Set sub-goals.
Breaking up your goal into sub-goals is really essential to staying motivated, particularly for larger goals that take a long time to achieve. Sub-goals help you recognise and celebrate when you've made progress.

3. Work through a plan of action.
Having a tangible plan of action helps you to stay focused. To create a plan, do the following:

- Once you've worked out your sub-goals, make sure you write them down and place them where you can see them.
- Include a timeframe. Deadlines keep you moving and help you stay motivated. For each sub-goal you have identified, write down a deadline to prevent yourself from putting things off or forgetting your goal.

Building trust

"Trust is built in very small moments."
Brené Brown

One of the young budding leaders I mentor had been very frustrated with her team leader. The team leader's approach to developing her team member's career, as well as working on day-to-day projects, was stifling. My mentee felt that when she asked for what she wanted at work, her team leader would agree, then nothing would happen. We discussed various approaches she could take to try to change what was happening for her at work. Over time, it became so frustrating for my mentee that she really was not enjoying work at all and it became a chore for her to go.

Fortunately, because she was a trainee, she only had to wait until a new rotation for a new team leader. I met my mentee a few weeks after her rotation and it was like she was a new person. Her enthusiasm was back. She felt that her career was developing. She loved the work she was doing and she was excited to go to work again.

During our mentoring session, we unpacked what made the difference between the two leaders. Essentially, my mentee felt that she could trust her new team leader, who was genuinely listening and understood what she wanted and needed in order to develop her career. Most importantly, she also felt that her day-to-day work was being designed around these requests. Her new team leader was doing what she said she would do for my mentee.

Trust is the basis of our sense of safety and dignity as human beings. It is one of the key ingredients for strong relationships – and a leader needs strong relationships with those around them to achieve outcomes.

A dictionary definition of trust is 'a firm belief in the reliability, truth, or ability of someone or something'.

In the book 'The Thin Book of Trust: An Essential Primer For Building Trust At Work',[21] Charles Feltman defines trust as, 'choosing to risk making something you value vulnerable to another person's actions'.

Feltman also says that it is difficult to talk about trust without addressing distrust and its consequences. He says that distrust is 'a general assessment that what is important to me is not safe with this person in this situation (or any situation)'.

Trust is assessed by people about you. You may believe you are being trustworthy and acting with the best intentions but this may not change someone's opinion of your level of trustworthiness. You can only influence this assessment by what you say and how you act.

Where trust has been established in a relationship, you feel hopeful, curious, generous and caring. You are willing to co-operate, collaborate, engage, communicate openly, share ideas, and are willing to look at your own actions. There are normal to elevated levels of oxytocin, the connector hormone. Your cortisol levels will be low when you are working with this person. You have full access to your thinking brain so that you can think clearly and act.

Where there is distrust, you believe that it is dangerous to trust this person, which results in feelings of fear, anger, resentment and resignation. Your actions are built around defending, blaming, complaining, judging, avoiding, withholding information and ideas, and justifying protective actions based on distrust.

The fear part of the brain, the amygdala, is primed for any sign of imminent danger. There are elevated levels of cortisol and adrenaline because you are preparing for fight, flight or freeze. Your thinking brain is less active and there is greater reliance on defence-related patterns for making decisions and taking action.

In the example I gave of my mentee, I could see the change in her behaviour after working with the team leader she trusted, rather than the one she distrusted. She was engaged and willing to work. Previously, she was reluctant to work, judging her team leader negatively and blaming her for her frustration with her work.

In Chapter 3, 'Know Your Playing Field' and in Chapter 11, 'Nourishment and Replenishment', I cover the importance of maintaining a healthy hormone balance. When we are surrounded by trusting relationships, our hormones react positively so that we are happy, engaged and enjoying what we do.

You can see that trust is such a critical ingredient for leadership. But how do we learn this important skill?

The best resource that I have discovered is a program called 'Anatomy of Trust', by Brené Brown.[22] It is available online for free through her website CourageWorks – www.courageworks. com. I would also recommend reading Charles Feltman's book, which I mentioned earlier in this section.

Brené Brown breaks trust down into seven parts with an anachronism – **BRAVING:**

1. Boundaries – *You respect my boundaries, and when you're not clear about what's okay and not okay, you ask. You're willing to say no.*
2. Reliability – *You do what you say you'll do. At work, this means staying aware of your competencies and limitations so you don't overpromise. You are able to deliver on commitments and balance competing priorities.*
3. Accountability – *You own your mistake, acknowledge it, apologise and make amends.*
4. Vault – *You don't share information or experiences that are not yours to share. I need to know that my confidences are kept, and that you're not sharing with me any information about other people that should be confidential.*
5. Integrity – *You choose courage over comfort. You choose what is right over what is fun, fast or easy. And you choose to practise values rather than simply professing them.*
6. Nonjudgement – *I can ask for what I need, and you can ask for what you need. We can talk about how we feel without judgement.*
7. Generosity – *You extend the most generous interpretation possible to the intentions, words and actions of others.*

(Reproduced with permission)

By understanding this framework of the elements of trust, it is much easier to understand distrust. It also gives you a language for discussing with someone why you feel distrust, and being much more constructive about the situation and its impact on you.

Imagine if my young mentee had have approached her previous team leader with specific examples of why she believed she could not rely on her to keep her commitments. Do you think this may have led to a productive conversation about what could be done differently?

Of course, it isn't quite that simple. There are many elements involved in having meaningful conversations about trustworthy relationships. However, having a clear understanding of how trust has broken down does simplify the process. It also allows forgiveness to find fertile ground, as well as providing a starting point to hopefully move the relationship to a more positive standing.

When we are relating to another and experiencing fear, our mind adds its own storyline to explain what is happening in that situation. If we allow that storyline to fester and grow, we become suspicious of every action that person takes. It's then much easier to think in absolutes. "This person never does anything right." "They always act this way."

I'm sure you can remember a situation where you have exaggerated someone's behaviour. If you had a conversation with them about what you thought was happening, and compared that to what was actually happening, your whole perspective about the situation would probably have changed. You might even have found that you were the one who had exacerbated the situation.

The reality is that most people have good intentions. They may not have your standards or they may not have your skills, but they mean well.

This is what Brené Brown means by the concept of generosity: always believe that someone has intended the best.

You should also remember that there needs to be self-trust as well. The above principles also apply to how you treat yourself in situations. For example, reliability: was I reliable? Can I count on myself to do what I commit to doing for myself?

These are your practice steps:

1. Study the trust breakdown provided by Brené Brown, and write some notes on what the seven elements mean for you.
2. When you next find yourself saying that you trust someone or don't trust someone, consider which of the seven elements were present or not present in the situation.
3. Find the words that you would use to discuss your reasons for trust or distrust with that person. Be specific about the elements of trust that you have determined.
4. Speak to the person and discover their reactions to your reasons for trust or distrust.
5. Note whether this process resulted in a more productive dialogue with them.

Bias busting

The Neuroleadership Institute has been looking at the issue of organisational unconscious bias for many years. The main challenge is that most biases operate unconsciously so it's hard to remove them from decision-making.

Awareness that unconscious bias exists is important for an

individual and a leader. However, awareness alone does not help you recognise the bias in your own thinking.

To illustrate, we required a new financial adviser for our business team and we undertook an extensive recruitment program to find the right person. The adviser who we employed eventually came to us by accident, after one of those conversations at a conference where someone said, "I know someone".

It was my task to find the right person for the role and our business. I interviewed this person and really liked her and believed that she would be a fit for our business. I was extremely excited because the search had been long and wide and this person seemed just right.

The final step of our recruitment process for candidates is the Instinctive Drives tool, which I mentioned in Chapter 1, 'Know Thyself'. My ideal candidate duly completed the questionnaire and I received the report. I was stunned to find that the person I was excited to employ had exactly the same characteristics as me. I mean *exactly* the same Instinctive Drives. Of course, we had different life journeys so we were different people. However, our approach to our work, how we went about tasks, and how we completed projects would be pretty much the same.

This is called similarity bias. We are all highly motivated to feel good about ourselves and to see similar people in the best possible light.

Fortunately, I was aware of this human tendency, so sought discussion with the Board of Directors on whether my unconscious bias was going to impact our business. In the end, we went ahead with the recruitment of the candidate, because this person was ultimately to succeed me with client advising. We believed having someone similar to me would be helpful for client accept-ance, which has proven to be the case.

This is a positive story. However, if the similarity bias con-tinues you may end up with ingroups and outgroups. Promoting and protecting the ingroup may become the tendency, resulting in something particularly harmful to organisations, especially if there is a negative perception of the outgroup.

Ingroup statement – "I can trust her; she comes from my hometown."

Outgroup statement – "I can't trust him; look where he grew up."

We all have our unconscious biases that are the filters through which we see the world. These have been formed over time since childhood because of our experiences and our per-ception of how the world works.

The filters are our safety network as well as our belief system about where we belong in the world – two very important human responses. Our unconscious bias is the default mode in our minds. It is part of our biology as humans.

In fact, roughly 150 cognitive biases have been identified.

The November 2015 'Neuroleadership Journal' article titled, 'Breaking Bias Updated: The Seeds Model™', proposes three steps that can be used that interrupt and redirect unconsciously biased thinking.[23]

These steps are summarised below:

1. **Accept** that we are biased by virtue of our biology.
2. **Label** the type of bias that influences a particular decision into one of five categories that the Institute has defined as **The SEEDS Model™**.

3. **Mitigate** using the right process from The SEEDS Model™ (The Model).

The Institute developed The Model to condense the over-whelming number of individual potential biases. It was developed by identifying the core neurobiological correlates associated with the key biases, and through trial and error, organising a framework that separated the biases into categories.

This easy-to-remember framework will hopefully allow executives, managers and leaders in organisations to quickly identify the major types of biases that can impact their decisions.

The Model divides the cognitive biases into five types:

1. Similarity
2. Expedience
3. Experience
4. Distance
5. Safety

Similarity bias
In my example earlier of Similarity bias, the Institute suggests at least three modifications to mitigate the detrimental effects of this largely unconscious bias. These are:

- Increase awareness in organisations of Similarity biases and in particular the ingroup/outgroup biases.
- Implement unbiased hiring strategies, team assignments and intergroup interactions across race, gender, age, disability, sexuality etc.

- Enhance communication, conflict resolution, and perspective taking.

We found in our business that having sessions about each person's Instinctive Drives and Character Strengths as set out in Chapter 1, 'Know Thyself', changed everyone's focus away from the outer personal characteristics to the inner.

For example, in our firm, everyone had 'honesty' in their top five Character Strengths. Focusing on this strength across our team meant that we could appreciate each other better for our innate strengths and abilities rather than our looks or social background, or even how we tackled projects.

Expedience bias

Expedience biases are mental shortcuts that help us make quick and efficient decisions. The downside to these decisions is that they may be based on incorrect judgements.

The example used in the November 2015 journal to explain this bias is as follows – 'You have $1.10, a bat and a ball. The bat costs $1.00 more than the ball. How much does the ball cost?'

Most people will answer quickly and confidently that the bat costs $1.00 and the ball costs $0.10. It is the fastest and most expedient answer that comes into the mind. This has been labelled the brain's System 1 that relies on fast, easy associations and intuition.

The answer the bat costs $1.00 and the ball calls $0.10 is WRONG! If the bat costs $1.00 more than the ball, then the ball must cost $0.05 and the bat must cost $1.05.

To derive the correct answer, we would have needed to use our brain's System 2 and do some mental algebra. Engaging System 2, fact-checking and correcting, is harder work, so if System 1 answers come more easily and feel right, then most people don't think any further.

If a workplace has an inherent culture of urgency, then decisions may be required to be made quickly. This may affect the quality of the decision. If we make judgements based on our quick intuitions about what is right or what we want to be right, there may be no deliberation, fact-gathering or assumption questioning. This may result in irrelevant, incomplete and even flat out *wrong* information guiding our decision choices.

So the mitigation for the Expedience bias is to have extensive fact-gathering, to review all the assumptions being made, and take time to deliberate.

Experience bias

Experience biases come from our brains inbuilt understanding of how the world exists. This assumption that our experience corresponds to reality is referred to as naïve realism. Our expectations, past history, personality and emotional state are just a handful of factors that impact our view of the world out there.

Cultural differences are an example of Experience bias. In the Western world, we use cutlery to eat our food. It can be confronting when you travel to other countries where everyone uses chopsticks, for example, or even eats with their hands. We can actually think the other cultures are crazy for their eating habits; however, once we experience eating in a different manner we realise that their way is fine – just different from our experience.

One of the most interesting Experience biases is the bias blind spot. This describes the fact that it is relatively easy to see the biases in others but not ourself. Our tendency is to rate ourselves less susceptible to biases than others and see our answers less biased than others.

In organisations, this can be mitigated against by having teams of people make decisions about projects or recruitment, rather than one person.

Another Experience bias is the 'false consensus effect' – or overestimating the extent to which others agree with you or think the same way you do. For example, if you prefer vanilla to chocolate ice cream, you are likely to think that more people in the general population have the same preference, whereas someone who prefers chocolate to vanilla ice cream has the opposite perspective.

Leaders cannot assume that others agree with their preferences. It is essential on any project that you seek input from many people on your team about their preferences and needs before making any decisions.

Distance bias
Distance biases come from the network in our brain regarding proximity. Unconsciously, we assign greater value to those things that we perceive to be closer to us, simply because they are close.

One example of this bias is the endowment effect – you value something more if you own it than if you don't.

There is temporal discounting as well. This is valuing things differently depending on whether they are available now vs. later. For instance, given a choice between $10 right now and

$20 paid out in a month, most people will choose $10 now, even though the investment return of $10 over a month to receive the $20 is more valuable in the long run.

Our evolutionary past may have required us to focus on immediate resources for survival; however, in the modern world the longer-term view may be more beneficial.

Distance bias can also mean you are more comfortable with focusing on your local area for sales or business than wider afield because you feel that you know the area better. This is a space-driven proximity bias.

Safety bias
Generally, our decisions are more driven by *negatives* than by *positives*.

This is another one of those evolutionarily adaptive human characteristics. The Institute Journal article explains that in early primitive life you knew that you would stay alive longer if you remembered more quickly that the snake would kill you than that the bunny was cute. Put another way, losing $20 feels a lot worse than finding $20, which feels good.

Because we are loss averse, our tendency will be to make a risk-averse choice if the expected outcome is positive, but make a risk-seeking choice to avoid a negative outcome.

Also, if something is framed as a gain or as a loss, it may change our decision-making process. For example, when choosing to take a risk to avoid a 40 per cent probable loss, or choosing to avoid a risky decision for a 60 per cent probable gain the outcome is the same – but we are more likely to be drawn to avoiding the 40 per cent probable loss.

It's often hard for you to give up on a project when you've invested a lot of time, money and training, even though the project is doomed for failure. One of the mitigations for this unconscious bias is to know your tipping point on any project. This was covered in Chapter 4.

Unconscious bias

Unconscious bias exists in all of us. As individuals and leaders, it is imperative that you understand this human tendency in great depth if you want to bust these biases. If your role as a leader is to bring out the potential in people to ensure the outcome of your projects, you need to understand everything about the people you lead.

The Neuroleadership Institute has developed a program called 'Decide – a Scalable Learning Solution for Breaking Bias in the Workforce'.[24] I'm not going to focus on this program in this book; I just want you to be aware that it is available, and I encourage you to look at it if you want to be an exceptional leader in an organisation.

You can be assured it consists of specific goals, coaching, feedback and lots of deliberate practice as per Chapter 7, 'Practice, Practice, Practice'.

These are your practice steps:

1. Study The SEEDS Model™ from the Neuroleadership Institute, as outlined in this chapter.
2. Practise awareness of situations that arise during your day that fit the elements of the model.

3. Consider how your bias may be affecting the decisions you are making during the situations that arise.

4. Decide if there are any changes necessary to your behaviour or decision-making.

Building collaborative, diverse and inclusive teams

It has been shown that organisations flourish and sustain when they have collaborative, diverse and inclusive teams. Better decisions are evident, along with better performance. There is a mindset of personal development for individuals as well as a mindset of innovation for the organisation.

My thoughts on how to go about creating a collaborative, diverse and inclusive team are set out here in this section.

As a leader of a team, your role will be to bring out the best of each person's potential so that the project you are working on is successful. You will be ensuring that every team member is benefitting through the process of achieving project outcomes. This is part of the Service Leadership model – my definition of leadership. The realising of your team's individual potential is intrinsically linked to the outcome of the overall project. This is a developmental mindset.

As the leader, you will want everyone working to their best capability so the first understanding is around the human needs that each person is going to bring to the team. The second understanding is that each person on the team will have different skills and abilities that will need to be developed. The team dynamic will constantly change as members of the team join and leave.

The first step, I believe, is to establish a culture built around trust. The different elements of trust shown in this chapter need to be discussed, accepted and acknowledged as the basis for the way each person in the team deals with each other.

Then there needs to be a culture of transparency where team members are encouraged to be aware of their personal strengths and weaknesses, and asked to adopt a developmental mindset for their contribution to the team. Education about unconscious bias is adopted so that the team can look at better processes for effective decision-making. Everyone will be encouraged to be aware of the concept of bias blind spot.

Always provide an orientation process for new team members that will allow them to integrate quickly so you don't have the ingroup/outgroup culture creeping into the team.

Everyone needs to understand the importance of feedback and seek it for personal and technical improvement. A culture of no blame and no shame should be adopted by acknowledging that mistakes and weaknesses are an opportunity for improvement, not an opportunity to castigate someone or point score.

An environment of constant learning is encouraged, especially around emotional intelligence and the neuroscience of human behaviour in social settings. We must become better at working together.

One of the models to consider is SCARF®. This model, developed by the Neuroleadership Institute, helps with collaborating with others. More information can be found in the *Neuroleadership Journal*'s article, 'SCARF® in 2012: Updating the Social Neuroscience of Collaborating with Others' (Vol. 4).[25]

This model looks at threat and reward responses for people

and provides a framework to help learn about how people will respond when they are collaborating in teams.

SCARF® stands for the following:

Status – Refers to one's sense of importance relative to others (e.g. peers, co-workers, friends, managers, leaders).

Certainty – Refers to one's need for clarity and the ability to make accurate predictions about the future.

Autonomy – Is tied to a sense of control over the events in one's life and the perception that one's behaviour has an effect on the outcome of a situation (e.g. getting a promotion, finding a partner).

Relatedness – Concerns one sense of connection to and security with another person (e.g. whether someone is perceived as similar or dissimilar to oneself, a friend, or a foe).

Fairness – Refers to just and nonbiased exchange between people (e.g. praise for acknowledgment of one's efforts, equivalent pay for equivalent work etc.).

I have not noted any practice steps for this skill. There is lots of training and study required to understand the social behaviour of humans. This would be my only recommendation – start your own research and study in this area.

Effective communication

"They may forget what you said — but they will never forget how you made them feel."
Carl W. Buehner

Words matter. Your manner of saying words matters too. Our body language carries just as much impact as, if not more than, our words.

The most effective method of communication that I have discovered is called compassionate communication or non-violent communication. This method is set out in the book, *Nonviolent Communication – A Language of Life,* by Marshall B. Rosenberg.[26]

This method consists of four components.

These are your practice steps that I have summarised from the book:

1. **Observation** – Observe what is actually happening in a situation. Listen empathetically to the person. Try to articulate what you either like or don't like about what the person is doing or saying that is impacting you. The challenge is to articulate this without any judgement or evaluation.
2. **Feeling** – How are you feeling in relation to what you are observing. You state how you are feeling about this situation.
3. **Needs** – You say what needs, values, desires are creating your feelings.
4. **Request** – Finally you request concrete actions that you would like, which will change the situation or enrich your life.

An example:

"When you haven't done the work you said you were going to do by when you said, I feel stressed, frustrated and disappointed. I need the work to be done when I've requested so that I can meet our client's expectations, but also to keep my own stress levels down in the process. When I make a request, would you please consider whether it is achievable by the timeframe I've requested and work towards the deadline set."

This is a very simple example. In reality, you would allow the person to explain their actions through this process. You may want to read the team member's ID to see what Instinctive Drives are at work. There may need to be some further discussion around the need for training in time management. You may also find that the team member's workload is too great. The team member may need training in how to say no and how to set realistic deadlines and meet them. You may need to consider the methods set out in SCARF® before and during the conversation.

Notice, however, that the dialogue in the example is about me and my observations and feelings. There is no judgement or evaluation about the person. There are lots of "I ... " statements.

It is extremely challenging to refrain from evaluating. Often, we use the language that we are already speaking to ourself in our own self-talk. Often, we use our own self-judgements about ourself to the situation.

I've included in the Resources section at the end of the book the lyrics of a song called 'I've never seen a lazy man' by Ruth Bebermeyer that illustrates the difference between evaluation and observation.[27] The Indian philosopher, J. Krishnamurti, once remarked that observing without evaluating is the highest form of human intelligence. I believe we need to become smarter at this to make working together more effective. We also need to become smarter at effective communication.

I would recommend learning about body language as well. In the example I gave, if my tone of voice was gruff and my body stance aggressive, the message received by the team member may well have been seen as an evaluation not an observation. This would have shut down the dialogue because the person would have felt threatened and therefore would not listen to my message at all.

Join a communication club

Communication is paramount for leaders. I would recommend you join a communication club, such as Toastmasters International, so that you can practise getting to the point and making your message matter.

This will help you have the confidence to use your voice to ask for what you want in all situations.

Better self-talk

Self-talk is your inner voice, the voice in your mind that says the things you don't necessarily want to say out loud. Most of the time you may not even realise that this is happening. Every emotion, thought and action results in a storyline in our mind.

Self-talk can be positive or negative, depending on your emotional reaction to a situation, and the practices you have adopted for your life. As humans, we are attracted to the negative because it is part of our safety network to keep us safe from threat. Everything in life has a down side so we can't ignore it. There are lessons in the negative as well as the positive. It is impossible to be positive all the time.

There are three things you can do that can help change the dialogue and direction of your self-talk.

These are your practice steps:

1. **Listen to what you are saying to yourself** – Make a conscious effort to take note of what you are actually saying to yourself in your mind. I have discussed better transitions in this chapter. When you are transitioning during the day, take the time to listen to what you are saying to yourself during these transitions. If you have a chance, write down the words and emotions felt.

2. **Monitor your self-talk** – Is your self-talk more positive than negative? Start asking questions of yourself such as:

- Is what I'm saying true?
- Is there actual evidence of what I'm thinking?
- What would I say to a close friend in a similar situation?
- Is there a more positive way of reframing this situation?
- Do I have the right perspective about what has happened?
- Can I change what has happened? If no, then accept the emotion and process the message. If yes, then look at what positive actions you can take.

3. **Change your self-talk** – Easy to say but challenging to do in the heat of the moment. With practice, these steps work though. For example, if you are saying to yourself – "I'll never be able to do this". Ask yourself, "What can I do now that will help me to be able to do this?" Try to avoid speaking in absolute terms – don't use words such as 'never', 'can't', 'should', 'would', 'could'.

We can be our own worst enemies, especially as we speak to ourselves. When I became aware of my own self-talk, I realised that if I had a friend who spoke to me as I was speaking to myself, I would probably disown them. You need to become your own best friend and stop sabotaging yourself and your life plans with destructive self-talk. Practise the above steps as much as you can until they become ingrained into your daily routine.

Better transitions

Life was more delineated in the past. Societal roles were very clear-cut and defined. Work was work and home was home. Now home and work overlap because of easy communication, and the ability to work from anywhere, so our days require us to quickly go from one task, role and environment to another and back again throughout our entire day.

Previously, we would have come home from work for a quiet drink before dinner or even gone to a bar on the way home. This would have created a clear transition from work to home, and allowed us to unwind and change hats. Now we have our electronic gadgets with us, constantly interrupting our day with messages from work, friends and family.

As a woman leader today, this is your reality. Yes, it is stressful. However, it does allow us to more easily combine our different roles, and it allows us to hopefully be across parenting and work.

We need to become smarter at coping with this enmeshment. Dr Adam Fraser has written a book called *The Third Space – Using Life's Little Transitions to Find Balance and Happiness*.[28] In this book, Fraser has pointed out the benefits of using a set process for every tiny transition in your day so that you more easily bring your best self to all parts of your life.

Certainly, we know what happens if we arrive at a meeting stressed and unprepared. For most of us, it is not an effective use of that time, and this results in negative emotions and can lead to negative self-talk.

Fraser's system is very simple and is another reason why I like it. Easy steps and concepts are simple to incorporate and follow in your day.

I have added a few of my own techniques to assist with these transitions. The steps are as follows:

1. **Reflect** – Every time you transition from one task, role or environment to another, take time to reflect on what story you are telling yourself. If it is a negative story, take time to process the emotions and move yourself back into a positive state. If you have time at this transition, you could jot some quick notes on emotions and words that you are experiencing for later processing and review.

2. **Rest** – Take the time to pause and allow yourself to be present again. A technique that I use may help at this transition point. It is BSL – Breathe, Smile and Laugh. Taking a breath brings your thoughts into the awareness of your body. Smiling and laughing are known techniques for tricking the mind to believe that you want to be happy. This trick gets the brain to trigger the 'happy hormones' to be secreted. This can feel like a rest when your mood lifts. Sometimes it may not be appropriate to openly smile and laugh, so just think about this. Even if it is a forced smile and laugh, the brain does not know the difference. It will start trying to facilitate helping you to feel positive and happy.

3. **Reset** – This is where you think about what is happening in the next space that you are going to enter. I especially think about the people who I am going to be with in this space and think about their good qualities and what I like about them. Of course, if it is with someone that you have negative feelings about, you may want to let these negative feelings go as well. Otherwise, you are likely to make evaluations about them rather than observations.

Fraser recommends making an intention for what you want to happen in this next space. I agree with this. I try to think about what outcome I want to achieve or what qualities I am bringing to this space.

I also make an intention for my day when I wake up in the morning. I take the time to visualise what I hope will happen during my day, thinking about the people I need to see and the discussions that might happen. I think about the most important tasks that I need to happen for work and in my personal life.

Every night, I try to reflect on the day and process my perspectives on my day. I try to be grateful for the connections I have made, what I've achieved and what I have in my life. Notice I said, "I try". Sometimes I'm so tired that I'm not capable of thinking at the end of the day. If this happens, I include this process in my early morning intentions.

Of course, you will find days that you are not capable of following this simple process. So long as you adopt it most of the time, I know you will have a more positive, productive and less stressful day.

Some other words of caution. Take control of your electronic gadgets. You don't need to be connected 24/7. Turn them off, especially at night. There is nothing that will require more urgency than you having a good night sleep. Choose when you look at your electronic devices, including emails. Our minds are not designed to multi-task, despite what women constantly hear. We can do it for short periods but after that our processing brain becomes burnt out. We only have so many tasks that we can do before we have mental fog.

Women tend to be good at sequencing not multi-tasking. We can assess all the tasks that need to be done and order them to obtain the maximum use of our time. We still need to do the tasks one at a time with complete focus to achieve the best outcome.

Turn off all alarms and reminders that are going to distract as well, especially if you are working on an important project. You will see in Chapter 7, 'Practice, Practice, Practice', that clear uninterrupted focus is required for deliberate practice so that the learning becomes part of your mind. The emphasis is on 'uninterrupted', so email alarms and task reminders are distracting and will interrupt the continued focus.

I would recommend that you read the book *Two Awesome Hours*, by Josh Adam Davis.[29] This book applies neuroscience to time management. Davis argues that it is not about getting more done faster, but rather, creating the best conditions for at least two peak hours of performance. He covers many of the neuroscience applications that I have discussed in this book and applies them to a daily routine.

Summary

- There are lots of skills discussed here in this chapter. Assess which skills are the most critical for you to learn right now and start looking at how you can incorporate them into your life.
- Some of them can be sequenced, e.g. join a communication club – this will lead to effective communication at the same time as helping your self-confidence.
- Revisit the 'Basic Steps' chapter and apply this process to your learning of the basic skills. Remember the skills here are only a starting point. You may well find or know more that you need to explore and learn. I have set out the ones that I have found to be critical in my leadership journey.

CHAPTER SEVEN

PRACTICE, PRACTICE, PRACTICE

"Action without vision is only passing time. Vision without action is merely daydreaming. But vision with action can change the world."
Nelson Mandela

My first experience at public speaking was at school, when I was coerced into being in the debating team.

I distinctly remember looking out into this hall, with people looking at me, and I just melted away with fear. There was not one coherent thought in my head. I was so nervous that every part of my body was shaking, including my butt cheeks.

From that day, that traumatic experience permeated every attempt I made to use my voice in public. I would start to sweat; my voice would tremble and my mind would go blank. This reaction occurred even if I just wanted to ask a question at a seminar.

This all changed the day I joined the Advance Toastmasters Club and began their public speaking program, which incorporates deliberate practice.

More about deliberate practice is set out in the book called

Peak: Secrets from the new science of expertise, by Anders Ericsson and Robert Pool.[30]

Ericsson was fascinated with whether our inherent talents meant that we became an expert or extraordinary performer because of those talents. If you are a good musician does this mean you will play at elite levels?

What he discovered was that talent plays only a very small part in whether someone is going to be an expert or top performer. Many, many hours of practice are needed to make someone great in their field. In fact, the right sort of practice, carried out over a sufficient period of time, leads to improvement in any skill.

This amazing discovery means that you can learn anything you want in life with deliberate practice. It definitely means that you can learn to be a leader with deliberate practice.

With the Toastmaster's deliberate practice process, I slowly learnt the skills of public speaking. I am still a member of the Advance Toastmasters Club because what Ericsson discovered is that without continued deliberate practice we don't improve. In fact, we reach a plateau and then our skills and abilities may actually decline. Constant practice is essential to maintain and improve skills.

Effective communication is one of the basic skills I consider essential for a leader, so I continue to remain in a Toastmasters Club. This allows me to practise my communication skills in a deliberate manner with appropriate support and feedback.

In this chapter, I want to encourage you to employ the process of deliberate practice to everything that I have discussed in this book. The reason for my encouragement is that learning happens in layers of continuous habitual processes. The creation of new neural pathways in the brain takes many hours of deliberate practice.

Of course, you will not be able to do it all at once. What I hope you will do is look at what you are trying to achieve on your leadership path and decide the most important steps you must take right now. Then look at the deliberate practice steps below and see how you can systemise a process of learning.

You may also want to look at the book, *Competent Is Not An Option – Build an Elite Leadership Team,* by Art Turock.[31] Turock has taken the concept of deliberate practice and applied it to leadership skills with many of these systemised for learning.

The important steps with deliberate practice

Ericsson argues in his book that deliberate practice is different from purposeful and informed practice because there needs to be a field of endeavour that is already reasonably well-developed, such as sports or music or dance.

He argues that there needs to be accumulated knowledge about the field in which you apply deliberate practice. I believe that there is accumulated knowledge in the leadership field. Turock has started by looking at applying these techniques to leadership.

Even if there isn't a well-developed body of systematic processes, I still believe that you can take many of the deliberate practice steps and apply them to your purposeful and informed practice for anything you may want to learn. I have also provided some compelling neuroscience which shows you why you may want to include this in your life.

Deliberate practice steps

1. Establish effective training techniques for the process you want to learn.
2. Find a teacher or coach who is familiar with how to develop the skills required to oversee your training.
3. Ensure that the steps require you to be just outside your comfort zone so that you are required to constantly try things that are just beyond your abilities.
4. Set specific goals that are tweaked by your teacher or coach to lead to the larger change required. Improvement keeps the motivation going so that you want to keep improving.
5. Deliberate practice must be deliberate. It requires your full attention and conscious actions. You must concentrate on the specific goal that you are trying to achieve when you are undertaking your practice activity so that adjustments can be made. You need to be looking for ways to improve as part of your practice session.
6. Deliberate practice involves feedback and modification of efforts in response to that feedback. This includes you monitoring yourself, spotting mistakes and adjusting accordingly.
7. Deliberate practice both produces and depends on effective mental representations. Mental representations help

with the monitoring of improvement in practice and in actual performances. Mental representations help take the process to the subconscious and they help implant the skill in the body. Refer below to the neuroscience about this step.

8. Deliberate practice nearly always involves building or modifying previously acquired skills. It is a step-by-step process of improvement. New skills are built on top of existing skills, leading to expert performance.

Mental representations and motivation to learn

Motivation to learn requires an element of unexpectedness for the reward centres in our brain. This is explored in the Neuroleadership Institutes Journal article titled *The Neuroscience of Total Rewards,* May 2016.[32] The article discusses a process called 'mental contrasting'.

Mental contrasting is when you connect your thoughts and images of fulfilling a wish, and then consider what needs to happen in the present reality to move towards that reward. Once our internal motivation is activated with the mental images of fulfilling this wish, we are more likely to exert efforts on other tasks as well.

For example, if you envision, in detail, yourself giving a successful presentation in a meeting, after which you feel proud of yourself and competent (so you focus on feelings of confidence, and a positive reception from the audience), you are more likely to consider what you need to do in the present. The obstacles you need to overcome in your current reality to make that successful presentation may be to overcome your nervousness, and be prepared. By imagining the contrast between the future event and the present, you are more likely to set aside time to prepare and practise, ask colleagues for feedback etc.

When reward regions of the brain are activated, especially when a reward is unexpected, we are motivated to learn from the situation and to continue to receive the reward.

Our brains are wired to direct attention to information that will help us to maximise rewards. By having a clear picture of what we want (desired future or outcome) and what we have (current reality), this sends signals to the brain that there is something wrong. When the brain perceives a threat to our wellbeing it musters our energy and resources, looking for situations to overcome this threat. You are then motivated to take action and remedy problems so that you can achieve your goal.

Your brain will start looking for the tools and resources that you need to achieve your goal so that the perceived threat has gone.

The sense of accomplishment that comes from mastery is a powerful way to tap into your domains of social reward. Believing that you can master any learning through experience and a growth mindset makes your learning happen.

Incorporating deliberate practice steps will take learning from the conscious to the unconscious. Remember my quote from the Aseo tribe in Papua New Guinea, "Knowledge is only rumour until it goes into the bones". Deliberate practice will help to make this a reality.

Leadership practice

I encourage you to look at every life opportunity to learn leadership skills. Even having a tough conversation with your teenage child is a leadership opportunity. It's an opportunity to practise effective communication by establishing trust and using empathy and compassion. It absolutely requires emotional intelligence because the frustration of dealing with their processes of growing up can be very taxing on your emotions.

It may be necessary for you to work part-time for the sake of your family. I encourage you to look for ways of being a leader in your community during that time so that you can practise your leadership skills.

I became the manager of my daughter's soccer team when she was in her soccer-mad phase during her teenage years. It was one of the most challenging leadership roles that I ever undertook. On the other hand, it was one of the most rewarding. I got to interact with my daughter and her other team members, as well as their parents.

Believe me, there is a lot of organisation and negotiation required to keep a teenage girls' soccer team happening. My daughter also saw my support for her firsthand. The best thing of all was that I could watch her interactions as well, and this helped me guide and mentor her through those very challenging years of development. It is amazing what you can learn when you have a car full of teenagers and the opportunity to listen to their conversations.

Leadership is about guiding and empowering others to

achieve a common goal. There are many opportunities in our community to practise being a leader. Just do it!

Summary

- Mastery comes through practice not talent. Anything can be learned by applying deliberate practice techniques, including leadership. Constant practice is also necessary to continue maintaining our skills and abilities.
- Mental representations of what we want to achieve are powerful. Our mind becomes involved in helping us to achieve mastery. This takes the learning from the conscious to the unconscious so that we can move onto further learning, then to mastery.
- Take every life opportunity to practise your leadership skills. Learning to guide and empower others to achieve a common goal requires lots of skills that need to be mastered. Constant deliberate practice is essential for maintenance of your mastery as well. Just do it!

CHAPTER EIGHT

A CALL TO ACTION

"We cannot all succeed when half of us are held back."
Malala Yousafzai

My research for this book indicated that both men and women believe that we need stronger women role models. It is certainly my belief too. Once the world sees stronger women role models in all walks of life, the unconscious bias causing gender stereotyping will change.

Public companies that have high numbers of women executives consistently perform better than those with fewer women. One study of America's Fortune 500 companies found that the one-quarter with the most female executives had a return on equity 35 per cent higher than the quarter with the fewest female executives. On the Japanese stock exchange, the companies with the highest portion of female employees performed nearly 50 per cent better than those with the lowest. This isn't because female executives are geniuses. It just means that the companies that promote women are innovative, listen to ideas, and so stay ahead of the curve in reacting to business opportunities.

When there are diverse teams in organisations and governments, better decisions are made. Our human unconscious biases are also lessened with diverse teams that reflect our society.

The economic and social impacts of ignoring half the population are enormous for the world. When women move into more productive roles, this helps to curb population growth and nurtures a sustainable society.

As I've said throughout this book, leadership can start anywhere. Being a mother is a leadership role. As women, we just need to see the leadership status in this role. As Dee Dee Myers, former White House Press Secretary, said, "I am endlessly fascinated that playing football is considered a training ground for leadership, but raising children isn't."

I always say that every parent deserves a seat in the United Nations because of the deft skills they apply every day. The amount of negotiation and compromise required to encourage a child to participate in daily life is enormous.

On top of this, you need to model for them the benefits of growing into a happy, healthy and participating adult. What an honourable leadership role!

Yet, because child caring has been traditionally a woman's role, it is not given the merit it deserves. Because we have traditionally been the carers and supporters, we have not been given the merit we deserve.

I'm asking every woman who reads this book to believe they are leaders and stand up and be proud of it.

I believe more active participation of women in leadership roles will change the dialogue for boys and men as well. As fathers, if they become more involved with caring for their children, perhaps they will not expect their sons to go to war or their daughters to remain uneducated. (We know that snuggling with babies increases oxytocin for men just as much as for women!)

My book is an intellectual discourse about becoming a leader – and I hope it guides you to your next leadership role.

That isn't enough though. Change for women needs to be happening faster. If you care about a better life for all women in the world, then I'm asking you to become an activist for women's rights everywhere. If you care about more sustainable communities for girls and boys, then I'm asking you to become an activist for women's rights everywhere.

We need to remember the power that we hold. We control $5 trillion of investable assets; we direct 80 per cent of consumer spending; we're more than half of the workforce.

Summary

What does this power that we hold look like? How can we use this for the good of everyone? I have listed a range of ideas here for you to act upon every day.

- Mentor other women.
- Sponsor other women.
- Honour other women.
- Praise other women to men and women.
- Amplify what other women say in meetings.

- Point out to others when they interrupt other women or ignore other women in meetings.
- Be proud of being ambitious, assertive and competitive just like men, and speak out when someone uses the words 'mean', 'loud', 'aggressive' or 'bitchy' to describe a woman instead.
- Only join businesses that have successful senior women executives and that have effective bias busting programs for all who work there.
- Buy from companies that promote women appropriately. Have a look at the app 'BUY UP index'. This is an app that helps you make your purchasing decisions from companies that have demonstrated commitment to gender equality.
- If you're able, fund other women's businesses through crowdfunding.
- Encourage other women to become politicians.
- Become a politician.
- Start your own business built on the principles of equality for all.
- Lobby for better and more affordable childcare.
- Lobby for effective flexible workplaces so that parenting and careers are honoured equally.
- Support other mothers who are grappling with combining being leaders with motherhood.
- Support men who are supporting mothers to combine being leaders with motherhood.
- Encourage men to support women in every role.
- Ask men to champion women.

- Raise your sons to understand equality in everything, including household chores.
- Raise your daughters to understand their equal rights and show them how to speak out effectively for these rights.
- Donate to not-for-profit organisations that support women all around the world, such as Oxfam and UN Women.
- Be an activist for women's rights in every country in the world.
- Speak out against violence towards women.

WOMEN AS LEADERS – THE WORLD NEEDS YOU!

SUSTAINING YOUR LEADERSHIP JOURNEY THROUGHOUT YOUR LIFE

CHAPTER NINE

DEALING WITH SOCIETAL NORMS

"Be the one who speaks out above the crowd when everyone else follows the norm."
Ritu Ghatourey

I've discussed many ideas in the first part of this book to help you move from a state of doubt to a state of knowing about your potential as a leader.

The challenge is to sustain this over your lifetime so that you continue to grow as a leader and a person. This chapter looks more closely at the hurdles you may find along the way – especially societal norms – and what you can do to overcome them. They require the most vigilance.

Whenever there is structural change in a society, or a microcosm within, there are some who struggle with that and cause unrest. When you step up and make change, you will be surprised where criticism comes from – and equally surprised at the support you will receive from unexpected sources.

This is a good time to remember some of my earlier strategies:

- Understand who you are, what you are trying to achieve, and most importantly, why you want to achieve it.
- Dial down societies expectations of you as a woman and person. Choose only to read, watch, listen and explore on social media, the topics that are going to reinforce your purpose and meaning.
- Build your personal team of supporters who will understand what you are trying to achieve with your life, and seek solace from them whenever you are feeling jaded with society.

Demand change

We need to be demanding good and affordable child care from our government so that if we choose to continue our careers and/or being leaders in our fields, this is available to us.

It was only possible for me to continue to grow my business and be an effective leader because I knew that my daughter was adequately, appropriately and affordably taken care of. This happened because her father was the stay-at-home parent during her early years, and we were able to source adequate and appropriate child care for her when he went back to work.

When I knew my daughter was safe, well and cared for, I could focus on what needed to be done as a business owner and leader.

We need to be demanding flexible working arrangements so that we can blend the essential parts of our life, family and worklife. Workplaces need to allow appropriate flexibility so that we can participate in our children's development together with our work requirements.

I was fortunate that I had my own business, so I created my own flexibility. I know I was a much more effective business operator because my daughter was well looked after. I also know that I was a better mother because I was a business owner and leader, as I could still pursue my career. I would not have coped very well being a stay-at-home parent.

Part-time work needs to be acknowledged without stigma as well. Often, if parents choose to work part-time so they can raise their family and hold onto their careers, they are considered less valuable in businesses, government and organisations. Because of their part-time working arrangements there are no formal processes to ensure that they are trained and promoted, regardless.

It is also important to demand that our media reflects gender equality. There is still a constant stream of biased imagery in all forms of media, which reinforces societal norms of men as the strong, protective providers and women as quiet, decorative, homemakers. Men are portrayed as the leaders and women the supporters. These stereotypical images mean that these unconscious biases are reinforced to our children.

When I was growing up, my mother was a businesswoman and an advocate for equal education for my brothers and me. However, in my teenage years, I was expected to wash and iron my own clothes for school, but my brothers didn't have to. When I quizzed my mother about this anomaly, she told me that they didn't have to because they would have a wife to do that for them one day. This was in the late 1960s/early 1970s.

One day, just recently in 2016, I was horrified to hear someone close to me say that she had told her son to stop crying like a girl. I'm sure she would have heard this saying in her family, but it is not appropriate, and women need to be vigilant about how they are raising their future men. This comment is of no value to both young girls and young boys.

One of my clients, who is an early childhood educator, told me about the different behaviours she has seen mothers adopt with their boys and girls under her care. She sees some mothers of daughters come into the centre with their young girls, who have their backpacks on their own backs. The little girls are then expected to unpack their bags and put their daily supplies where required **and then go to play**.

Some mothers of boys, however, would come into the centre carrying the bag *for* their son and would then proceed to unpack the bag and put their son's daily supplies where required. Their sons, however, would just go off to start playing – totally unaware of their responsibility.

It is these subtle behaviours that continue to foster unconscious biases about the role of women. It is these subtle behaviours that eventually result in boys becoming men who are not as aware of their responsibility for their own wellbeing as they should be. It is these subtle behaviours that reinforce that women are expected to be homemakers, not leaders. It is these subtle behaviours that continue to make it challenging for women to be accepted in roles where the important decisions of the world are made.

Support women

I don't know how many times I hear stories about women who have failed at being leaders, and it's women who are telling these stories. I'm not saying that women don't fail. I'm not saying that women should ignore other women's failures, especially if it is impacting their work and their life.

I am asking that we acknowledge the courage that these women have displayed by being prepared to go into the leadership arena. I am asking that we don't stand on the sidelines and throw crap at their efforts. This only makes good women want to walk away.

If you know of someone who may have 'tried and failed', look for ways you can find out more about them and see if you can step in to support them. Your efforts may not be accepted initially, especially if you come with an attitude of shame for their failure. So, step in with your most generous attitude and see what you can do to support them.

Men have had thousands of years in leadership roles. Women have had a few decades. We are still learning the skills required.

Look for examples of women's success and honour and praise them. Tell other women and men about these women. Tell your daughters and sons about them too.

I was recently at a work meeting and we were looking for advocates for our new service line. Two of the men present were going through their male contacts. They could remember all of the career moves that these men had made, and showed enormous respect for their successes. I don't think I've ever heard other women having the same process – including me. These men were honouring their colleagues for their success. We need to be doing the same for women.

Follow the careers of the women that you admire. Acknowledge and honour their journey to other women and men, and your daughters and sons. This is how we can ensure that strong women are identified, accepted and expected in our community.

Encourage and support men

Encourage men to be open to and interested in the idea that you want different options for your life. Encourage them to be involved in the caregiving for your children and other people in your family. Ask men to be your champion at work and to endorse your ideas and processes.

Remember that we have been doing the caregiving for thousands of years, whereas men have only been doing this for a few decades. They are still learning the skills required.

Also, they may or may not have different processes to you. It doesn't matter, as long as the solution is the same.

Not everyone is going to like you and you are not going to like everyone

As women, we are expected to be nice, friendly and accommodating – typically a supporter. When you step into a leadership role, not everyone is going to like you because you may need to make decisions that are not going to please everyone. You will need to step in when people are not meeting expectations of their role; and not everyone will have sufficient emotional intelligence to deal with negative feedback.

If you adopt some of the techniques I have discussed in this book, you will ideally mitigate others losing trust in you. Hopefully you can maintain respect. Everyone does not have to like each other. You may not wish to have some people at your Christmas dinner. As long as there is enough trust and respect for people to work together to ensure the project 's success, that is all that matters.

Men seem to have a much better understanding of this than women – perhaps because they have had more practice.

My point is that sometimes it can be a lonely journey as a leader of a project. When this happens, look to your support network for validation.

Summary

- Societal norms about gender will take many generations to change. Work out your own methods of coping with unreal expectations of you as a female leader.
- Demand the changes that you need so that you can combine your leadership role and your other personal roles, such good and affordable child care, flexibility in working environments and respect for part-time working.
- Be vigilant about societal messages that reinforce gender stereotyping and demand changes.

- Support women to be leaders by stepping into the arena with them where appropriate. Find out their stories and have a generous view of what they are trying to achieve. Follow strong women's careers and tell their stories to your family, children, friends and work colleagues. Honour women's courage as leaders.
- Encourage men to understand why you want to be a leader and ask that they support you on that journey. Support them in their caring roles and have a generous view of how they undertake this role.
- Leadership can be a lonely journey because you may have to make decisions that not everyone is going to like and appreciate. Look to your support network for validation whenever you are experiencing this. Strive to ensure that trust and respect are maintained wherever possible.

CHAPTER TEN

MANAGING 'THE BIG SQUEEZE'

"Start where you are. (Again and Again.)"
Pema Chodron

The strategies I have discussed in this book sound so practical and simple on paper. The challenge comes when you start to include them in your life, business or home. Often reality does not match vision or intention. This is what I call 'The Big Squeeze' – the disparity between thought and action – between vision and reality – between wanting and achieving.

When discussing unconscious bias in the chapter on 'Knowing Your Playing Field', I mentioned my friendship with Bridget during my primary schooling. Bridget and I had many discussions about how we thought we could change the world. I'm sure that if I had recorded those conversations, they would sound very naïve and unrealistic. I also remember many hours at university spent debating the state of our world and what needed to happen to improve it.

Looking back on those times, as I write this book, I consider whether my vision for the world as a young person is dramatically different from my vision for the world now.

Yes, there is frustration that there is still a long way for us to go as humans, to ensure that everyone has a good life and our planet is protected. When I look back on what has been achieved though, I'm staggered at the progress. There are deadly diseases, such as polio and tuberculosis, that we have eliminated from the world within my lifetime. Abject poverty has been decreased for many of the world's population. Fewer women die in childbirth and fewer children die in childhood. We also have readily available contraception so that women can choose the size of their family. We've walked on the moon and explored more of the universe.

Now we have internet that provides instant information on everything – I had to wait for books to be sent to the Barcaldine Library to read such information when I went to school with Bridget.

We have technology that means I can sit here and wait for my Canadian friends to FaceTime me so I can see them in real time. I used to have to mail pen pal letters when I was at school, and then wait many weeks for a response, and maybe a photo if they could afford a camera and the cost of processing.

The reality is, we are never totally satisfied. We are always looking back at what could have been, and then looking forward to what we want to achieve. We are constantly restless to move on to the next adventure, learning and life experience. This constant yearning though distorts our present moments – and our present moments are all we have.

I recall when I finally received my qualification as a Chartered Accountant. It was about 11am when our results were pinned on the noticeboard at the Institute of Chartered Accountants (as it was known then) in Sydney. We all traipsed to one of the buildings to receive our results and those of us who saw our name on the list went to celebrate, while those whose names did not appear went to drown their sorrows.

It was a lot of fun celebrating. But by mid-afternoon another emotion came over me and I asked myself, "What's next, Denise?" I became quite down, realising that I had finished what I had wanted to achieve and it appeared that there was nothing else in front of me. Yes, crazy I know. I'm sure there was an element of the alcohol affecting as well. I no longer drink alcohol because I came to realise, later in my life, that alcohol was too much of a depressant for me. It colours my life with blue and black rather than a rainbow. I prefer rainbows.

Summary

So, here are my suggestions for managing 'The Big Squeeze':

- Look back regularly and relish achievements. Our tendency is to see the negative first. Don't do this with your life. Dial down the stumbles, the dead ends, the failures and the deviations from your plans. As you review your life, you will see that you were in the right place at the right time for the right learnings.
- Celebrate every moment. Learn to stop and relish this moment and the experiences that are around you and within you right now. If ever there is a compelling reason to learn mindfulness meditation, it is this. We don't

know when our last moment is to occur. Do you want your last moment to be obliterated by negativity, yearning and what-ifs? I know I don't.

- Have plans for the future, but detach yourself from them. Visions of what you want to achieve are important, however they are just mental representations. They are not reality. You need to detach from the outcome so that you can enjoy the journey, which is a collection of many moments as you move towards a goal. If you are fixated on an outcome and it doesn't eventuate as per your mental representation, you are likely to be disappointed. This will colour your future even more.

- Sit with negative emotion and find the learning. If you are disappointed at the outcome of a plan, be still with the emotion and explore it. Realise that there are a lot of other people who are probably experiencing the same emotion as you at this moment. This strengthens your empathy and compassion muscles. Find the learning in what happened and see if you can apply a different approach in the future. Perhaps you just need to persist a little longer – or maybe the plan did not realistically suit.

- Don't get hooked by the emotion. Both positive and negative emotions are fleeting, unless we feed them. If you find yourself caught up in negativity, do something different. Take a deep breath and connect with your body, smile and even laugh. Find the words associated with the emotion and journal them. Go for a walk, or meet a friend for coffee. (This also applies to positive emotions. Don't let them feed your false sense of self-importance.)

- Try not to get self-righteous about anything. No one person has all the answers. You certainly don't know everyone's story. Unless you lived their life, you cannot know why they have made the decisions they have. You can study their behaviour for pointers for your own life. Don't be judgemental though. Encourage the people around you to do the same.

- Failure is not a dirty word. Try to see failure when it happens (and it will) as an opportunity. Try not to feel that because you have failed that you are a failure as a person. Yes, it is ok to be disappointed and upset at what has happened. There are many learnings in failures. These are the opportunities. If you read most stories of success, you will find that there were failures before success showed up, and some of the failures were spectacular. Don't let your fear of failure stop you from doing anything.

- Remember that when you add something into your life, something else may have to be removed or reduced. We only have so many hours in a day. We only have so much energy in a day. The best example of this happening is when you find your life partner. You want to be with them a lot! Suddenly, there is less time for your close friends and other family members. So try to work out what will change when you decide to add something like projects and leadership assignments to your life, and consider the impact and how you will manage this change.

- Life is a gift. Be grateful every day for what you have in your life. Of course, you can aim for and expect more but don't forget what you have already.

These are a few of my methods for managing The Big Squeeze. Look for your own and use them regularly in your life.

CHAPTER ELEVEN

NOURISHMENT AND REPLENISHMENT

"Body, like the mountain
Heart, like the ocean
Mind, like the sky"
Dogen Zenji

Living is easy. You breathe in, you breathe out. Living so that you feel you have squeezed every ounce out of yourself, your day and your life is challenging. It is also exhilarating, empowering and tiring all at the same time.

Throughout the first section of the book I have mentioned the times I have almost come unstuck – literally and figuratively. These times happened when I forgot to take care of myself.

Being a leader is like being the conductor of an orchestra. You are bringing together all the elements of sounds produced by the orchestra members and their instruments, and creating a complete work of sound art that will touch the souls of the listeners.

If you are sick or unwell, or even just tired, your beat may be out of sync with others, and this will disrupt the flow of sound.

Fortunately, if you are part of a team, other team members may pick up the rhythm and run with it for a while.

It is essential though that you be self-centred, especially when it comes to your own health and wellbeing. Your team, your family and your life will run for a while without your direction, but not forever.

Also, when you are strong physically, mentally and emotionally there is a flow that happens, which somehow makes everything seem easy. It would be fabulous to exist in this state permanently, but unfortunately it waxes and wanes just like most things in life, and it takes consistent effort.

As discussed in Chapter 1, 'Know Thyself', your consistency will come once you have discovered what works for you and what makes the flow happen.

Consistent does not mean 'marathon runner'. Of course, if you have the time and ability to be a marathon runner and it is what lights up your life, then go for it. If you have a career and you are a leader, plus you have a life partner and family, it may need to be as simple as a 20-minute walk around the neighbourhood with the family dog.

Consistent means realistic and achievable, with some aspirational element thrown in if possible, for example: "I'm going to walk twice this week and three times next week."

I love combining things to make maximum use of my time. When my daughter was little, we would walk to the park for her to play. My exercise would be walking around keeping her safe, plus appreciating her efforts, which she loved. Sometimes, if I was lucky, I would have five or ten minutes to myself to enjoy the park and relax.

The one consistent exercise that I have always enjoyed and love having in my life regularly is swimming. Most people find it boring swimming laps, but I find that I combine my mindfulness meditation time with the swimming actions. The sound of my breath is so definite, rhythmic and consistent in my head when I swim. It is very easy to focus on these sounds, as well as the floating feeling in my body, and the rhythmic strokes. I find this clears my cluttered mind for this period so I can just focus on my body and the individual thoughts that arise. (I actually found myself de-stressing as I wrote this passage!)

If something is consistent, that means when life intervenes, you will go back to your physical exercise routine as soon as you can.

Scientists have proven that physical exercise is the key to mental and emotional health as well, so I want to emphasise the importance of consistent physical activity in your life. You may find at various times in your life and leadership journey that you don't have time for learning new ideas or mindfulness meditation. That's fine; just don't compromise on the physical exercise. Find what works for you and ensure it is scheduled into your week!

We need good fuel to be energetic; healthy eating is important. When we have low blood glucose we have a lower ability to make quality decisions and we are challenged to self-regulate our emotions. Sometimes when we are busy, we don't feel like eating or we think we don't have time to eat. My experience has been that this rebounds on me later because my energy levels drop rapidly and it takes quite some time to restabilise.

The biggest contributor to mental fatigue is lack of sleep, so good sleep is critical. I know that if you have young children, good quality and length of sleep can be challenging to achieve. When these times occur, you may have to lighten your work-load or be more mindful of how you are travelling during the day. Neuroscientists are finding that even a 20-minute (maximum) nap can recharge the batteries. I have tried this and it does work.

Another important part of nourishment and replenishment is incorporating time out in your life, and includes holidays. It is very easy to be sucked into a daily routine that just keeps repeating itself – over and over again. There can be an element of comfort in the sameness of the routine, but our minds need freshness for creativity. Remember, insight comes when the mind is quiet and relaxed.

Also, when you are combining leadership and parenting, your day is enmeshed with work and family, which starts from the minute you put your feet on the floor in the morning until you put your head back on the pillow at night. Our technology today also facilitates this enmeshment. Text messages, emails, Facebook – these can be responded to from the toilet!

Our minds are not designed for this constant bombardment of images, information and decisions. This barrage makes the mind feel like it is under threat constantly, which sends the body into alert mode, sending out adrenaline and cortisol ready for flight or fight.

Research is showing that mindfulness meditation is a won-derful tool to provide that window of 'time out' in a day. This practice is taking 10 to 15 minutes of your day to sit, be still and just focus on the breath. It is a technique to quieten the mind.

You cannot stop thinking. The mind is designed to think. The aim of mindfulness meditation is see your thoughts and become aware of the quality of them.

When adrenaline and cortisol are high, thoughts can be scattered, obsessive and anxious. With mindfulness meditation, you can observe these thoughts and with practice even notice the impact on your body – your shoulders have risen and are tight, your tummy is full of butterflies, your thighs and buttocks are tight and clenched.

You can practice mindfulness meditation anywhere and at any time. It can even be done in the toilet; although, if you are a mother your children will follow you there as well!

If you are challenged to find 10 to 15 minutes for yourself to do this practice, I would recommend having a mindfulness app on your phone. Set up regular reminders that just give you a minute to take a deep breath and regroup, or become aware of your thoughts.

My technique is BSL – Breathe, Smile and Laugh. Sometimes, depending on where you are, it is not appropriate to smile and laugh, but you can still imagine you are doing this. When you smile, your mind believes you want to be happy and will start to send out serotonin to escalate the change in mood to positive.

We are emotional and biological creatures, and for every emotion we experience, we add our own storyline. Positive emotions motivate and make us happy. Other times the storylines are dramas, sometimes tragedies; and often they can be self-destructive. You know the ones – 'you are fat', 'you should have done this', 'you should have said that', 'who are you to think they will listen to you?'

Becoming aware of what story you are telling yourself is liberating. Once you know what that is, you can question the thought. You can reframe a negative to a positive. Mindfulness gives you a mechanism to ensure good quality thoughts. It also gives you the mechanism to bring you back to the present moment.

As leaders and mothers, we determine the mood of our team and our children. Sorry! Yet, another responsibility on your shoulders. If you want your team to show up authentic, optimistic and high-energy then you will need to show up consistently with this attitude. If you want your children to be positive, happy and calm, then you need to consistently show up with this attitude. The good news is that the two are not mutually exclusive. By this I mean that your leadership qualities flow into your motherhood and vice versa.

Take the time to find tools that work for you that allow you to be authentic, optimistic and calm, and don't compromise on including them in your life. Ask for support from your team and your family so that you can incorporate these tools into your calendar. Your team and your children will appreciate that a happy leader or mother is much better than a frantic and anxious leader or mother.

What I have discovered also is that because I'm happier and calmer, my immune system is strong and so I rarely become ill with colds and flus. This means I can take more time to exercise and meditate, which means my immune system is strong, which means that I am calm, happy and positive – and around it goes.

I have appreciated discovering Dr Adam Fraser's book, *The Third Space*. He added another tool to my kit by providing some techniques to look at the smaller transitions in the day. As discussed in greater detail in Chapter 6, his idea is that when you are transitioning during the day from one task, role and environment to another, that you follow a set process so that you enter the second space in the best way possible. The process is called 'Reflect, Rest and Reset'.

I believe that armed with 'Reflect, Rest and Reset', together with 'Breathe, Smile and Laugh', your day will go well and you will be able to squeeze every ounce out of life, for you to enjoy.

Summary

- As leaders and/or mothers, you set the scene. If you are authentic, positive and calm then your family and/or your team will be too. To achieve this state, you need to find life tools that suit you and that you can incorporate into your life to achieve this as often as possible.
- Physical exercise is paramount for overall wellbeing, including mental and emotional health. If you don't have time for anything else, try to always include physical exercise in your week in some form or other.
- Good fuel from good food and the right amount of sleep are important to stop mental fatigue, ensure good decision-making and to help with self-regulating emotions.
- Be self-centred about your 'me time'. Ask your team, family and friends to support you with your endeavours to stay physically, mentally and emotionally healthy.

- Look at taking regular time out in your day, week and life, including holidays. Consider incorporating mindfulness meditation into your life. If you are challenged with the meditation, then explore mindfulness.
- Incorporate the micro-transition techniques of 'Reflect, Rest and Reset' when you transition from one task, role and environment to another. Remember to 'Breathe, Smile and Laugh' as well.
- Schedule your life tools into your calendar with your other important meetings, tasks and agendas, and don't compromise on this. You are the most important person in your life so don't cancel a crucial meeting with your most important client.

FINAL WORDS

"Life is either a daring adventure or nothing!"
Helen Keller

This book is for aspirational women who are seeking the daring adventure of being a leader. It is not definitive, as it has touched on many topics.

I hope I have provided enough stimulating information to influence you to start or continue your journey as a woman leader. I hope I have given you enough insight into how you can sustain your leadership journey throughout your life.

We must become smarter at interacting with each other – it is crucial to us all living meaningful and joyful lives on this planet, our only home.

I believe women must play an essential role in making that happen. I'm asking you to see yourself as a leader and step up and do it.

Women as Leaders
The World Needs You – Start Today!

ABOUT THE AUTHOR

I am the Founder of Integrity Wealth, which is a small full-service boutique financial services business in Brisbane, Australia.

This business grew out of my sole practitioner accounting business that I purchased suddenly in 1992. I was in partnership then with a gentleman named Warwick King, who had built the business – a genuinely gentle, honourable man.

It was Warwick's intention to retire gracefully over a number of years but unfortunately he was diagnosed with cancer in 1992, and passed away. Three weeks after he passed away, I fell pregnant.

So I inherited a baby and a business. Motherhood and business combined – an amazing mix.

But how did it all start? After completing my Commerce degree and a Postgraduate Diploma of Advanced Accounting at the University of Queensland in Brisbane, I started my accounting career with PriceWaterhouseCoopers (PwC, formerly Coopers & Lybrand) in Sydney. The initial four years of my career were spent with PwC in Sydney and Perth. I followed this with almost four years at a mid-sized firm of accountants at Crows Nest in Sydney.

I became a Chartered Accountant in 1980, while I was with PwC.

During these eight years, I also went back to the family home in Barcaldine, Queensland, for a ten-month period to look after my mother who died of bowel cancer. Our family had two businesses in the town, so not only did I look after my mum, but I assisted with the management and operation of these businesses, as my mother had been a key person in their management.

During my last four years as an accountant in Sydney, I met and married my now ex-husband. We decided to move back to Brisbane because it was a long way from Sydney to Barcaldine to visit my dad.

I met my business partner, Warwick King, almost immediately after arriving back in Brisbane in 1984. I started working as a contract accountant for his three-partner accounting firm at Capalaba in Brisbane.

There were many twists and turns in business and life from 1984 to 1991, for both Warwick and me; however, in January 1991, we finally became business partners and the firm was called W G King and D M Gibbons Public Accountants.

Warwick was the first male business colleague who genuinely believed in my abilities as a business person and a female leader, and he openly promoted me to all and sundry.

There had been other men throughout my career who had believed in me and given me business opportunities or encouraged me to keep going. However, Warwick was the first one who became my male champion as well as my mentor and friend. It has been the most empowering experience of my career to date.

After Warwick died and my daughter was born, I put the business on hold while my daughter was little so that I could work flexibly around her development. Her dad became the stay-at-home full-time carer. We did use day care for her from six months as well, so my husband could continue his business as a cabinet-maker. He needed his work for his sanity just as much as I did.

The first five years of my daughter's life were the most exhausting of my life. I think this is the same for any parent.

In our case though, we were older parents, both with businesses and 11 years of being just the two of us. What a culture shock! No one can prepare you for it either. You just have to live through it.

There is so much learning that happens through that process though that does genuinely help you with life. You learn so much about yourself and that makes you grow as a person. You become resilient, resourceful and patient (well, most of the time) in between bouts of total insanity and exhaustion.

This is the same for any caring role. I had the same experience looking after my mother.

The difference with parenting though is that you are dealing with a child, so the responsibility is greater and the caring is unrelenting. You have to be everything for them until they are an adult – and that could take 25 years. Ahhhhh!

My daughter is 23 now and she has grown around my business. I know this was very frustrating for her at times but she has grown into a very strong and determined young person, so I don't think it has done her too much harm.

I grew up around my parent's businesses and I know it didn't do me any harm. If anything, it made me very worldly from a young age. Also, I saw firsthand the satisfaction of being part of making things happen in a community.

This was probably the start of my addiction to adrenaline; the adrenaline that comes from the challenge of making a business run efficiently and effectively. Once you have experienced this, you are hooked for life.

I also became a financial planner in 1998, to ensure that the business became a full-service financial services business, as I could see that this was how I could best serve my clients. And it has been during those 24 years with my business partners that I have successfully grown the business to be just that. There is an extended family of about 20 people involved to varying degrees with the business now, and I have two business partners, Mark Stewart and Samara Badgery.

Once I started expanding the business, my leadership learning began. Learning to motivate a group of people to achieve a common goal requires lots of formal and informal skills. If you want to be a leader you have to be prepared to learn these skills.

I am now entering a new phase of my business life as I transition from ownership with Integrity Wealth to a consultant role so that I can pursue other endeavours, including running women's leadership courses. I know that I am leaving the business in good hands with Mark and Samara.

It is a wonderful feeling to know that I have created such a successful and sustainable business, which impacts many lives.

RECOMMENDATIONS, RESOURCES AND REFERENCES

INTRODUCTION
Reference:
1. Toastmasters International High Performance Leadership Program definition of Service Leadership – www.toastmasters.org.au

HOW TO USE THIS BOOK
Resources:
2. Honestly Woman Magazine – www.honestlywoman.com
3. Leadership Programs with Denise Gibbons – www.denise-gibbons.com

WHAT IS LEADERSHIP AND WHY BECOME A LEADER
Reference:
4. Toastmasters International High Performance Leadership Program definition of Service Leadership – www.toastmasters.org.au

CHAPTER 1 – KNOW THYSELF

Resources:

Websites:

5. Instinctive Drives – www.instinctivedrives.com

6. Character Strengths – www.viame.org

Book:

7. Britton K and Polly S, *Character Strengths Matter – How to Live a Full Life*, Positive Psychology News, LLC 2015.

References:

8. Gawler I, 'Exercises for reclaiming your life' from the book, *The Mind that Changes Everything*, Brolga Publishing 2013.

9. Ware B, 'Most common regret – I wish I'd had the courage to live a life true to myself, not the life others expected of me' from the book *The Top 5 Regrets of the Dying*, Hay House Australia 2012.

10. Brown, Brené, 'Shame triggers and shame resilience' – www.brenebrown.com
    - *I Thought It Was Just Me (But It Isn't)*
    - *The Gifts of Imperfection*
    - *Daring Greatly*
    - *Rising Strong*

CHAPTER 3 – KNOW YOUR PLAYING FIELD

References:

11. UN Women – National Committee Australia, *Rethinking merit – Why the meritocracy is failing Australian businesses*, May 2015.

12. Neuroleadership Institute Journal, *Breaking Bias*, May 2014.

13. Gladwell M, Podcast, *The Lady Vanishes* – www.revisionist history.com

14. Proceedings of the National Academy of Science (PNAS) Journal, *Father's brain is sensitive to childcare experiences* by Abraham, Hendler, Shapira-Lichter, Kanant-Maymom, Zagoory-Sharon and Feldman, 8 July 2014.

15. Fraser Dr A, *The Third Space – Using Life's Little Transitions to Find Balance and Happiness*, Heinemann 2012.

16. Neuroleadership Institute Journal, *An Ideal Hormone Profile for Leadership: Can you Help Yourself be a Better Leader?* by Josh Davis and Pranjal H. Mehta, March 2015.

17. Cuddy A, TED Talk – *Body Language Shapes Who You Are.*

CHAPTER 4 – KNOW YOUR TIPPING POINT
Reference:

18. Brown, Brené – *The difference between empathy and sympathy*, YouTube https://www.youtube.com/watch?v=1Evwgu369Jw& list=PLt7b6WnSW1ynvTqyu3l_WnAEMhMmwXYl6>

CHAPTER 5 – BASIC STEPS
Resources:

19. Toastmasters International High Performance Leadership Project

20. Leadership Programs with Denise Gibbons – www.denise-gibbons.com

CHAPTER 6 – BASIC SKILLS REQUIRED

Reference:

21. Feltman C, *The Thin Book of Trust: An Essential Primer For Building Trust At Work*, Thin Book Publishing 2009.

Resource:

22. Brown, Brené, 'Anatomy of Trust' – www.courageworks.com

References:

23. Neuroleadership Institute Journal, *Breaking Bias Updated: The Seeds Model*™, November 2015.

24. Neuroleadership Institute program, 'Decide – a Scalable Learning Solution for Breaking Bias in the Workforce'.

25. Neuroleadership Institute Journal, *SCARF® in 2012: Updating the Social Neruoscience of Collaborating with Others*, Volume 4

26. Rosenberg MB, *Nonviolent Communication – A Language of Life*, Puddler Dancer Press 2010

Resource:

27. Bebermeyer Ruth, *I've never seen a lazy man*

I've never seen a lazy man;
I've never seen a man who never ran
while I watched him, and I've seen
a man who sometimes slept between
lunch and dinner, and who'd stay
at home upon a rainy day,
but he was not a lazy man.
Before you call me crazy,
think, he was a lazy man or
did he just do things we label "lazy"?

I've never seen a stupid kid;
I've seen a kid who sometimes did
things I didn't understand
or things in ways I hadn't planned;
I've seen a kid who hadn't seen
the same places where I had been,
but he was not a stupid kid.
Before you call him stupid,
think, was he a stupid kid or did he
just know different things than you did?

I've looked as hard as I can look
but never seen a cook;
I saw a person who combined
Ingredients on which we dined,
A person who turned on the heat
and watch the stove that cooked the meat –
I saw those things but not a cook.
Tell me, when you're looking,
Is it a cook you see or is it someone
doing things that we call cooking?

What some of us call lazy
some call tired or easy-going,
what some of us call stupid
some just call a different knowing,
so I've come to the conclusion,
it will save us all confusion
if we don't mix up what we can see

with what is our opinion.
Because you may, I want to say also;
I know that's only my opinion.

References:
28. Fraser Dr A, *The Third Space – Using Life's Little Transitions to Find Balance and Happiness*, Heinemann 2012.
29. Davis JA, *Two Awesome Hours*, HarperOne 2015.

CHAPTER 7 – PRACTICE, PRACTICE, PRACTICE
References:
30. Ericsson A and Pool R, *Peak: Secrets from the new science of expertise*, Dolan Harcourt 2016.
31. Turock A, *Competent Is Not An Option – Build an Elite Leadership Team*, self-published 2015.
32. Neuroleadership Institute Journal, *The Neuroscience of Total Rewards*, May 2016.

9 780995 446403